THE BEST OF BRITISH BUSES

Nº6 A E C REGALS

ALAN TOWNSIN

TITLES IN THIS SERIES

First Published by Transport Publishing Company Ltd in 1982
This book exclusively reprinted for BOOKLAW/RAILBUS TRANSPORT EDITIONS December 1993

BOOK LAW
TRANSPORT EDITIONS
RAILBUS

Designed, typeset and produced for the Publishers by
Mopok Graphics, 128 Pikes Lane, Glossop, Derbyshire
Printed and bound in Great Britain

Contents

FRONT COVER ILLUSTRATION

City of Oxford Motor Services Ltd was a regular and almost exclusively AEC customer during the period covered by this volume,
batches of front-engined Regals being added to the fleet in most
years between 1931 and 1940 and again in 1949-50. The vehicle
shown here had been one of the last batch of nine on the Regal
Mark III 9621A chassis with 9.6-litre engine, 'crash' gearbox and
Willowbrook 32-seat bodywork, placed in service in 1950. Although
withdrawn by Oxford in 1963, all nine were purchased for further
use by other concerns and this one was subsequently restored to
the traditional and distinctive red, maroon and duck-egg green
livery. It is seen about to leave Belle Vue, Manchester on a Trans-
Pennine Rally in the late 'seventies.

Introduction

Competition was keen through most of the production life-span of the vertical-engined AEC Regal in its various forms, but the model was always a serious contender for the leading position in its market. It may well have been top of the full-sized six-cylinder single-decker hit parade in terms of numbers built at various times during its first couple of years of production from the autumn of 1929, since the totals of both the Leyland Tiger, its arch-rival (and design cousin), and the Regal were around the 1,100 mark for that period. Admittedly Leyland's total share of the single-deck market was practically doubled by the addition of an almost similar number of four-cylinder Lion models but the Regal's only other serious rival among six-cylinder chassis was the lighter and cheaper Gilford 168OT, much favoured by independent operators, but about a couple of hundred short of the Tiger or Regal's total in numbers sold over the same period.

However, the Regal never caught up with the Tiger's total of vehicles in service, at first because the latter had been on the market two years earlier. Though the Gilford challenge collapsed after 1932, the Tiger assumed new importance with its widespread adoption as the standard for numerous company fleets in all parts of the British Isles. The Regal never quite regained its original market position, despite a wide range of alternative specifications including early diesel and epicyclic gearbox variants, partly because of delay in developing a suitably compact and efficient diesel engine. Attempts at broadening the range with the four-cylinder Regal 4 and the lighter Regal Mark II were only marginally successful, though there seems no clear reason why the Regal 4 did not do better in the pre-1934 period, save perhaps an instinctive customer reaction that Leyland, or for that matter Tilling-Stevens or Dennis, had a better reputation with earlier four-cylinder models.

The 7.7-litre direct-injection engine was effective enough when it arrived on the scene, helping to restore the Regal's commercial position, but London Transport's preference for the 8.8-litre for its 1938 fleet of 266 Green Line coaches tended to confuse the issue, excellent machines though they were to prove, as well as forming the largest order yet.

The immediate post-war Regal I of 1946-47, simple and rugged with the '7.7' engine, was just what operators needed to get back into normal peacetime business and sales were well up — but then so were those of most makers. With hindsight, the Regal III in its original 9.6-litre engined form, with what at the time was an advanced combination of air-operated preselective gearbox and air-pressure brake operation, was perhaps a little too complex to have a large-scale following as a 35-seater — the situation was very different in the double-decker field.

There was, in any case, a tendency by big operators to hold back to await the introduction of the underfloor-engined models known to be in course of development and the Regal III only briefly held the position of being the standard single-decker choice of relatively limited numbers of company fleets in Britain. It had been designed as an export vehicle to an extent far greater than any previous Regal variant (with particular emphasis on the development of a true left-hand version) and this became its role to an even greater degree after 1950, despite the availability of 30ft.-long home-market versions when such vehicles became permissible that year.

It was not until the era of the underfloor-engined Reliance in the mid-'fifties that AEC again became a market leader in the single-decker field to an even firmer extent than had been the case in 1930-31, but that is outside the scope of this volume.

So the Regal was, overall, on the fringes of large-scale commercial success and only intermittently achieving the volume sales at or near market-leader level. In view of AEC's position as primarily a city and

This photograph of a Regal in the fleet of the Bath Tramways Motor Co was taken in 1935, but the vehicle shown was one of the first dozen of the model to be built, supplied to Plymouth Corporation towards the end of 1929 [see also overleaf]. The idea of using a six-year-old vehicle for a publicity photograph was almost unheard of in those days of rapid change, yet apart from the rather square-cut Mumford bodywork, DR 5807 still looked suitably up-to-date, a measure of the way in which the Regal set the standard in terms of styling, during that period.

hence double-decker bus builder, it does not seem surprising, in retro-spect. And many of the smaller makers of the period would have been glad to emulate its sales quantities in even the leanest years.

In terms of design trends, the Regal had immense influence. The original 1929 version may have derived much of its mechanical design from the 1927 Leyland Tiger, understandably in view of both being the work of G. J. (John) Rackham, but the Regal and related models certainly set the standard for appearance with their deeper and slimmer radiator set flush with the front dumb-irons and compact use of front-end space. The list of other manufacturers influenced by this front end design could be quite a long one, but clear echoes could be observed in the products of Bristol (from 1931 and such models as the H and J), Daimler (with the CG6, CH6 and CP6), Dennis (the Arrow), Leyland (from 1933 and the Tiger TS6), the TSM era of Tilling-Stevens, and Thornycroft (with the Cygnet) quite apart from several smaller concerns such as Vulcan.

Basingstoke, 1982   Alan Townsin

5

The first AEC Regal, chassis number 662001, was one of twelve delivered to Plymouth Corporation in 1929. It is seen here after being in service for a year or so. The radiator is of the same style as fitted to the first dozen of the corresponding Regent double-decker model, with less rounded outline to the grille each side of the triangular name badge than standardised thereafter. The front hub cap is of the 1930 pattern, however, possibly as a result of substitution. The bodywork, seating 32, was built by W. Mumford Ltd of Plymouth, who were also AEC distributors for Devon and Cornwall. Plymouth had not been a major AEC customer, although some single-deckers had been supplied in the mid-'twenties, and Leylands were favoured subsequently, the Regals being sold in the early 'thirties though most saw many further years of service with the Bath Tramways fleet.

Chapter One: Origins and background

When George John Rackham was persuaded to return to AEC, as Chief Engineer, after an absence of twelve years, in the early summer of 1928, his principal concern was probably the double-deck market. The company's position as a subsidiary of the London General Omnibus Co Ltd implied close involvement in city bus manufacture, as did his own success, just beginning to bear fruit, with the original Leyland Titan double-decker he had designed and seen go into production during his two years at Leyland. He had also been largely involved in double-deck bus design in his previous position, again as

Chief Engineer, with the Yellow Coach Manufacturing Co Ltd in Chicago.

Yet the position in regard to single-deckers was equally in need of urgent attention. AEC, whose full title in those days was the Associated Equipment Co Ltd, was ending the two-year spell when its vehicles had been sold under the name of the Associated Daimler Co Ltd (often abbreviated to ADC) which had been set up as a joint sales concern with the Daimler Co Ltd. Lord Ashfield, Chairman of the Underground group then responsible for most of London's public transport system (including

LGOC) was also Chairman of ADC.

The plans for manufacture of vehicles with a choice of AEC or Daimler engines at AEC's new factory at Southall to the west of London had not worked out particularly well and Daimler had resumed manufacture of complete single-deck chassis at the end of 1927, though the resulting vehicles had been sold under the ADC name as models 423 (with forward control) and 424 (a bonneted model).

AEC's contribution to ADC's single-deck range, the 416 and 417 models (again forward and normal-control respectively) had by no means

Typical of AEC single-deckers in the period just after the break-up of the ADC regime, this 426 model was one of several supplied in November 1928 to F. Duffy of Cork, in the Irish Free State, as it then was. This concern had quite a sizeable fleet, using the fleetname 'General' then more familiar on buses of AEC's parent company, the London General Omnibus Co Ltd, though there was no connection with that organisation. The bodywork, by Strachan and Brown, was of a design also popular on similar chassis in England. The 426 had a four-cylinder side-valve engine offering no more than adequate performance even by contemporary standards — the curious lack of maker's nameplate on the radiator meant that there was no external difference between examples of this model built under the ADC or AEC name.

Rackham's first step in the updating of AEC's single-decker range was the incorporation of his new 6-type engine in a slightly modified 426 chassis, the end result being called the Reliance. The new engine had a thoroughbred appearance entirely in keeping with its character even in production form, as shown here — prototype units had more polished aluminium. Note the oil pressure gauge, intended purely for under-bonnet inspection.

been a flop, with some 987 of the 416 model built in 2½ years from its introduction in 1926, plus 124 of the 417. Admittedly some had Daimler engines, but most of the big orders for 416-type buses specified the four-cylinder side-valve AEC 4-type engine. These vehicles had a fairly squat radiator typical of the period but the Daimler-built 423 and 424 had a somewhat slimmer style very like that on contemporary Daimler cars (except for the lack of the characteristic fluting) and this was also used on new face-lifted versions of the AEC-engined 416 and 417 designated 426 and 427, introduced at the beginning of 1928.

These last were AEC's sole offerings at the time of Rackham's appointment. They were still selling, but not as well as the 416. Competition was particularly strong by this date, as manufacturers saw the opportunities of rapidly expanding

bus and coach services. Design development was also very rapid, and what had been seen as a good contemporary design in 1926 was already becoming dated.

Rackham had himself created what was to prove the most successful of the new more powerful six-cylinder single-deck models in the form of the Leyland Tiger introduced with and in design very similar to the Titan double-decker revealed at the Commercial Motor Show in November 1927, but the 426 model's most direct rivals were the Tilling-Stevens Express, the Leyland Lion PLSC (of pre-Rackham design), and such models as the Dennis E, the Albion 30/60 hp series and the Bristol B. These all had four-cylinder petrol engines, generally of much the same size as the 426's 5.1-litre unit, but of more up to date design. In particular, the continued AEC use of splash lubrication for big-ends

limited speed and engine life between overhauls. There were also several other six-cylinder models beginning to make a reputation for themselves, and in particular Gilford's policy of combining American-built engines with light chassis design was already successful in terms of sales.

So action was urgent and although Rackham's thinking was, as usual, broad enough to cover a complete range, it was decided to produce a stop-gap single-decker with a new engine he put in hand immediately on arrival at Southall, in what amounted to the 416/426 chassis. This was the original Reliance, model 660, announced in January 1929 although at least one example had been delivered in November 1928.

The new engine, given the generic classification '6-type', owed much in its general design to Rackham's design for the Leyland Tiger and Titan, with six cylinders, overhead

Comparison between the stop-gap Reliance chassis (left) with its mid-'twenties characteristics and the new Regal (facing page) reveals their markedly different design, apart from the common factor of the engine. The graceful curves of the Regal frame gave lower stresses, with maximum depth where it was most needed. The Reliance had a cone clutch, apt to be decidedly fierce in take-up and amidships-mounted gearbox with a rather ponderous right-hand gear lever whereas the Regal had a very smooth-acting plate clutch and unit-mounted gearbox. The Regal chassis, very probably the first one, had been photographed before the bonnet was fitted and had not yet received the petrol tank, though this was mounted on the right as standard.

camshaft layout and seven main bearings with, of course, pressure-fed lubrication, giving outstanding smoothness as well as much better performance. It was slightly smaller in swept volume, at 6.1 rather than 6.8-litres, but was slightly faster revving and gave a directly comparable power output. This was generally advertised as 95 bhp, almost twice as much as the 4-type engine in the 426 which gave only about 50 bhp, so greatly improved performance was available. AEC now had a coach capable of running at up to 50 mph or more, highly illegal though this was in relation to the official general speed limit of 20 mph.

However, while the Reliance was helping to create a new image for AEC as a manufacturer of high-performance vehicles, work was

nearing completion on the new range of chassis. These were to be named Regent, Regal and Renown, being respectively two-axle double-deck, two-axle single-deck and three-axle models with model type numbers 661, 662 and 663 respectively. All were of closely-related design, particularly in regard to the Regent and Regal which differed only in such matters as springs and tyre sizes to suit different loading of double- or single-deck bodywork and numbers of passengers, and in length.

At first the 662-model Regal had a 17ft. wheelbase, being intended for bodywork with an overall length of 26ft., whereas the Regent was respectively of 15ft. 6½in. and 25ft. dimensions. Visually, the Regal chassis differed from the Reliance 660 most noticeably in its gracefully

curved frame profile linking the areas where the sidemember level was raised over the axles to the lower level between them and the rear. In fact, the design was new in virtually every detail, again having much in common with Rackham's previous designs for Leyland and to some extent, Yellow Coach.

A smooth-operating single-plate clutch replaced the Reliance cone unit which had possibly been that model's most dated feature, with its tendency to fierce engagement. The new four-speed gearbox was mounted directly behind the engine instead of amidships and had a modern-style gear lever mounted alongside the engine instead of the right-hand gate-change arrangement that was another obsolete feature of the previous model. Both models had

Despite its somewhat dated chassis design, the Reliance's new engine made it an effective contender in the highly competitive market for single-deckers. Its smooth-running engine was well suited for coach operation, and the performance available with 95 bhp on tap for a vehicle weighing only 5 tons 2 cwt unladen as in this example was quite lively even by the standards of 50-odd years later. Glenton Tours Ltd of Lewisham was also to become a regular customer for the much later genera-tion of underfloor-engined AEC Reliance coaches. This example, placed in service in 1929, had folding-roof bodywork of the type still quite popular at that date — note that the driver had his own cover which could be opened or closed independently. The body is believed to have been by Redhead of Lewisham, whose name can be read on the transfer below the driver's step on the original photograph.

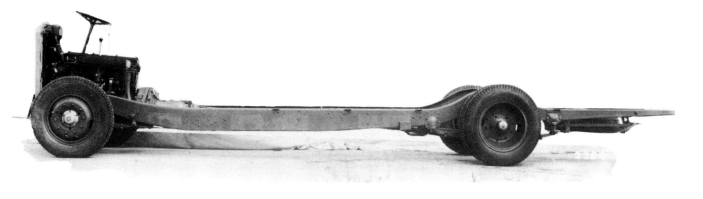

This photograph of an early engine, radiator and gearbox assembly dates from about the same period, around the early summer of 1929, as that of the complete chassis above. It illustrates the way in which the radiator was mounted directly on the engine and the whole assembly carried by the front cross-tube and the pressed crossmember behind the engine.

This bodybuilder's drawing of the Regal chassis appeared in the first catalogue relating to the model — it is reproduced here to a scale of 4 mm to 1ft. It reveals that although the original wheelbase was standardised at 17ft. 0in., alternate chassis lengths to suit 26ft. or 27ft. overall lengths were offered. It is also noteworthy that the chassis is shown without either front or rear dash panels, though most Regals and Regents were supplied with these for incorporation into the bodywork, the main exception being the LGOC and associated companies and, later, London Transport, who thus had greater freedom in the shaping of the bodywork in these areas. The dotted outline of a typical cab roof [shown to indicate where sockets for lifting eyes for the cylinder head and gearbox were to be provided] indicates that overall height was expected to be only about 8ft. Low build was fashionable at the time, although only a limited proportion of bodywork, mainly coaches, was as low as this, and overall height tended to creep up subsequently.

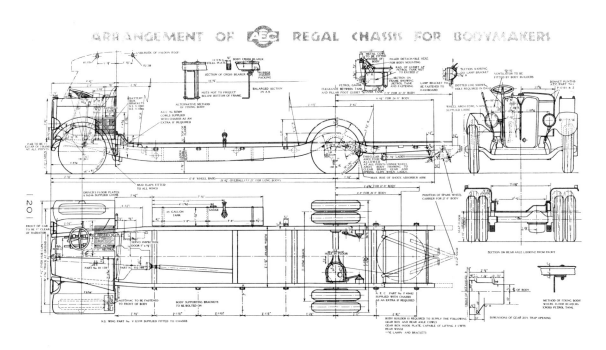

worm-drive rear axles, but the Regal unit had the differential casing offset to the nearside. This was a feature of particular importance on the Regent double-decker which used the same unit (apart from a change of standard axle ratio), but it also enabled the Regal's gangway level to be as low as possible. Low build was a selling point for all types of passenger models at that period and coach bodywork was often built to as low an overall height as possible.

The development of the vacuum servo had allowed power-assisted braking to become a standard feature of Southall-built passenger models during the ADC period and the Regal had, at first, a single-servo braking system using mechanical linkage to the front and rear axles — four-wheel brakes had also appeared in the ADC era.

Where the Regal and Regent broke new ground was in their front-end layout and external appearance. AEC had pioneered a compact forward-control layout in 1919, during Rackham's absence, with the K-type double-decker and the basic idea of mounting the radiator at the extreme front of the chassis frame had been followed on all subsequent models. Rackham took this principle to its logical conclusion and was able to save 6in. in 'bonnet length' (or more precisely the length from the extreme front of the chassis to the front bulkhead) as compared to his Leyland designs of a couple of years earlier, despite basically similar engine dimensions.

Of equal importance for the coach market in particular, the Regal set new standards of appearance. The slim-framed radiator, with its subtle curves embracing the distinctive triangular badge, made most existing designs look dated and its proportions, with the lower edge extended downwards to line up with the lower edge of the dumb-irons, added to the up-to-date appearance. Competitive makes had little option but to imitate, sooner or later.

During the spring and summer of 1929 a total of twelve Regent double-deckers were built and bodied before being sent to various operators to gain operational experience. The first dozen Regal models, with chassis numbers 662001 to 662012, all went to a single operator, and were evidently built later in the year but some of them had the same style of radiator, slightly different from the subsequent standard and they may thus also have been in the nature of a pre-production batch.

The London General Omnibus Co Ltd, in those days AEC's parent company, was the first operator to place a large order for Regals, the 50 chassis concerned being supplied in the autumn of 1929, all but one being fitted with LGOC-built 30-seat bus bodywork and entering service by January 1930. The rather square-cut body design was neatly proportioned and did not look unduly dated when most of the last examples were scrapped in 1953 — their appearance had not greatly altered apart from livery changes [despite most being rebuilt from rear to front entrance in 1930-35 and eighteen of them being refurbished by Marshalls of Cambridge in 1949]. T30 is seen here as operating in early London Transport days.

The lively performance and good handling qualities of the Regal were soon appreciated by drivers. This 1930 example with London Lorries bodywork in the fleet of Blue Belle Motors Ltd is seen hurrying through Hyde Park on that concern's Paddington-East Grinstead service, with conductor signalling for the benefit of the driver of the mid-'twenties Bean car following, though he'd have to put his foot down to keep up. The East Grinstead service, together with four similar Regals, although not this particular one, was taken over by Green Line Coaches Ltd. The Regals subsequently became T346 to 351.

Chapter Two : Early production Regals

The first big order came, understandably, from the LGOC. This was for 50 chassis, 662028-77, to which the bonnet numbers T1-50 were allocated in sequence. They were intended for suburban bus services and most were completed, with rear-entrance 30-seat bodies built at LGOC's Chiswick works, in November-December 1929. There were, however, two significant exceptions to the standard design. The chassis of T38 was diverted to form the basis of a coach and was effectively the first Green Line vehicle, though not painted in that livery at first.

More radically, bus T43 was originally fitted with an experimental in-line eight-cylinder engine, reputedly similar in general concept to the standard Rackham-designed 6-type but of smaller cylinder bore (87 mm) to keep the swept volume roughly the same as the 100 mm-bore six. Because of contemporary limitations on length, the body was 6in. shorter than standard to compensate for the longer engine. After about a year the vehicle, along with four double-

deckers with the same type of engine, was rebuilt as standard.

Unfortunately no photographs of this engine or the complete vehicles in their original form appear to have survived. It would be interesting to know whether there was any significant gain in smoothness over the already excellent performance of the standard engine. Fascinating though it was, this exercise can only be regarded as an engineer's indulgence, for the standard Regal proved from the start to be both refined and reliable, appealing to a wide variety of operators.

Some were already established as regular AEC customers. Elliott Bros of Bournemouth, in those days the proprietors of the Royal Blue express service network, had been a major user of the Reliance so it was hardly surprising that the same name appears in the lists of early Regal operators, including chassis number 662017. Another very early Regal, 662020, originally an AEC demonstrator registered MY 2276, was to find its way via the Watford Omnibus

Co into London Transport's fleet as T371, thus becoming nominally the oldest T-class vehicle. Chester Corporation was another early municipal customer, its chassis 662027 and 078-86 straddling the LGOC order.

But it was the independent operators, especially in and around London, whose names were sprinkled liberally over the early order lists. AEC's success in selling chassis to independent operators was particularly noteworthy in an era when, as a subsidiary of the LGOC, the concern might have been considered as unacceptable as part of an organisation that was often regarded as the major threat to the independents. There was a certain irony in the fact that many of these Regals were taken over by London Transport after that organisation had been set up with monopoly powers over regular services within the greater London area in July 1933 — a few were actually taken over by the Green Line Coaches Ltd subsidiary of LGOC in 1932-33.

When combined with the vehicles

Ireland was quite an important market for AEC around 1930. This Regal was supplied to Rocksavage of Cork and is believed to have been quite an early chassis, 662026, which was registered PI 5168, later passing to the Irish Omnibus Co and thence through the hands of the Great Southern Railway fleet to Coras Iompair Eireann, where it remained in service until 1947.

built for LGOC subsidiaries, notably the Green Line, East Surrey and Autocar fleets, the proportion of vehicles eventually included in London Transport's fleet from early Regal production was high. The total of chassis built in 1929-31 was a little over 1100 and 306 of these (with fleet numbers T1-306) had been supplied new to LGOC or Green Line (mainly the latter). Vehicles acquired as a result of the formation of the LPTB took the fleet numbers up to T402 and all but sixteen of this total also dated from 1929-31, thus accounting for about 35 per cent of production.

The remainder included some sizeable numbers of vehicles owned by London area independent operators not subsequently involved in the LPTB take-overs, notably such concerns as A. Timpson of Catford. Sales to major area companies were not at first particularly numerous — the Leyland Tiger had established a firm hold on that market, though East Midland Motor Services Ltd took ten in 1930 and 20 in 1931 and modest numbers went to such concerns as Devon General, Rhondda and Western Welsh while the Scottish Motor Traction Co Ltd took delivery of the first batch order for eleven vehicles in what was to prove one of the largest Regal fleets.

Several municipalities placed orders and the Regal seemed to appeal to operators on both sides of the Pennines, such as Huddersfield, Halifax and Burnley, although quantities were relatively limited as most fleets were tending to concentrate on double-deckers, often for tram replacement. Early overseas business came in from South America (later to become a major export market for Regals, even if one early vehicle sent to Lima Transport in Peru in 1930 bounced back, later becoming London Transport's T369 via the Watford Omnibus Co Ltd), Stockholm, Spain and India, where Regals were supplied to the Bombay Electric Supply Co and the Maharajah of Patalia.

Don Everall of Wolverhampton was representative of early independent operators to favour the Regal, though the choice of a fully-fronted body style was unusual. This vehicle, UK 8450, dated from early 1930.

[Above] Elliott Bros [Bournemouth] Ltd, proprietors of the Royal Blue network of express services covering the south west of England, were natural customers for the Regal, having 25 Reliance coaches already in service as well as converting six 426 models to Reliance specification with 6-type engines. However, one example each of the Regal, the Daimler CF6, the Leyland Tiger and the Maudslay ML6 were placed in service in the winter of 1929-30 before placing an order for eighteen Regals and nine Daimler CF6. The Regals arrived in June and July 1930, all having Duple bodywork of the distinctive style shown, modern in outline for that date, though the shape of the skirt panels with multiple mouldings was to give them an unusual appearance. When Elliott Bros sold out to Tillings in 1935, the fleet was divided between the Southern and Western National companies, which continued to run the Royal Blue services, and Hants & Dorset, which took over the excursions and tours side of the business based at the former headquarters in Bournemouth. The vehicle shown, LJ 1512, chassis number 662143, went to Southern National and, like most of the others, was rebodied, in this case in 1938 by Duple and remained in service until 1953.

[Below] When AEC printed its first catalogue for the Regal in 1929, United Automobile Services Ltd was listed as an authorised AEC distributor for Norfolk and the part of Suffolk covered by a twelve-mile radius from Lowestoft, [where the company also had its bodybuilding works], as well as for Bishop Auckland, County Durham. Thus when Harrison & Ives Ltd, trading as Eastern Motorways, of Norwich, placed an order for a Regal coach for delivery early in 1930, it was logical for it to have United bodywork. VG 2284 had chassis number 662201 and the styling of the 26-seat two-door body design was similar to that on United's own fleet of contemporary Leyland Tigers, though it perhaps suited the Regal even better. The Eastern Motorways business was taken over by United on 1st October 1930, but the United organisation itself was split the following year as a result of its purchase by Tilling & British Automobile Traction, its operations in East Anglia together with the Lowestoft bodybuilding works being transferred to the newly-formed Eastern Counties Omnibus Co Ltd. United's association with AEC as distributors ceased. This vehicle was included in the transfer to ECOC; it retained its United fleet number KA48. This photograph clearly shows the 1930 style of front hub cap, with blue and red centre.

Varsity Express Motors Ltd of Cambridge operated express services between London and both Oxford and Cambridge. After purchasing Gilford coaches in 1929, an order for AEC Regals was placed, the vehicle shown, 662266, being the first of three with 28-seat bodywork by Dodson supplied in 1930. Two more with Duple bodies followed later in the year and three more with bodies by Dodson in 1931. The business was taken over by Eastern Counties Omnibus Co Ltd in August 1933 but in April 1934 the London-Oxford service was transferred to the United Counties Omnibus Co Ltd, together with all but two of the Regals. They were rebodied by Burlingham in 1939, VE 3031 received a 31-seat coach body, remaining in service until 1950. United Counties operation of this service, far removed from its base in Northampton, continued until after South Midland Motor Services Ltd came into the Tilling empire in 1950.

A. Timpson & Sons Ltd of Catford, also in those days an independent concern, specialised on large company outings as well as running a thriving business carrying individual passengers on coastal excursions. A regular contract was that conveying the staff of Kennards, a Croydon department store on its annual trip to the seaside. Eight of the fleet of 20 Regals with Harrington bodywork placed in service in 1930 are visible in this view as the convoy heads for the south coast, and another operator's Regal, possibly hired in to assist, is just visible behind. The leading vehicle, GC 4820, had chassis number 662174.

The Western Welsh Omnibus Co Ltd had been founded under the unlikely-sounding title for a bus operator of South Wales Commercial Motors Ltd in 1920, but was expanded considerably in 1929 following the acquisition of an interest by the Great Western Railway. New vehicle orders were split between Leyland and AEC in the next years, the first for the latter being for twelve Regals in 1930, the first vehicle, No. 553 [UH 8621] on chassis 662462, being shown in service bound for Ammanford. Bodywork was by Northern Counties, the style of cutaway rear entrance being more often associated with the practice of some Scottish operators but also being favoured at that time in some Welsh fleets. Note the steam wagon in the background.

[Above] Samuelson New Transport Co Ltd of Eccleston Place, Victoria, London, had been operating daily express services since the mid-'twenties to the Midlands and these were extended to Liverpool, thus becoming involved in the strong competition covering London-Liverpool services. This Regal glistened in the sun soon after being placed in service in 1931 — note the side route board ''London-Shakespeare Country-Liverpool''. The company was acquired by London Coastal Coaches Ltd, the operators of Victoria Coach Station, in 1936 and its services transferred to associated companies though a small fleet was retained for private hire.

[Below] The distinctive silver and blue livery with 'gothic' Silver Service fleetname of J. H. Wooliscroft & Son of Darley Dale, Derbyshire, was found on a variety of AEC models over the years. This Regal dating from early 1931 had a service bus interior but incorporated a roof-mounted luggage carrier. RB 3954 had a quoted unladen weight of only 4 tons 12 cwt. The bodywork is believed to have been by Cravens.

Municipal orders for Regals formed a relatively small part of the total output in the early days of the model, but Huddersfield was one of several undertakings in hilly areas on both sides of the Pennines to put batches in service, doubtless influenced by the good performance over such terrain. No. 77 [VH 3291] on chassis 662456 was one of seven examples with Hall, Lewis 32-seat bodywork delivered in 1930.

[Right] Hills in Somerset were also no stranger to Regals. AEC made effective publicity use of this picture of 662224, Western National 2963 [YC 9727] with Strachans 32-seat body taken when climbing the famous Porlock Hill en route to Lynmouth, well laden with passengers and luggage. The picture was taken in July 1935 and illustrates how a 1930 Regal was still considered as being not unacceptably dated in an age when styling tended to change quickly — indeed, the vehicle would have been regarded as quite old by contemporary standards of life expectancy.

[Below] No doubt suitably refreshed after a call at the Whoop Hall Inn, passengers board a smart new 1931 Regal in the Progress Motor Services fleet of W. Armitage and Sons Ltd of Blackpool bound for Huddersfield, where this operator also had a garage. FV 1687, on chassis 662622, was one of four Regals supplied through Oswald Tillotson Ltd, AEC's wholesale distributors covering most of the north of England. The Burlingham body, a Blackpool product, was one of a style produced in both coach and bus variants.

[Above] Now and again when looking through official photographs one comes across a mystery. Why did Leyland Motors' official photographer take this picture of two Regals with Burlingham bus bodies in December 1930? They were in primer and no doubt in course of delivery from the Burlingham coachworks in Blackpool, perhaps to Oswald Tillotson Ltd at Burnley, which concern sold similar vehicles to quite a number of operators. They may have been for stock and hence not finish-painted. It may have been the recently-introduced body design that was of interest but one wonders whether Leyland design staff were looking into competitive vehicles with a view to introducing revisions to update the Leyland range.

[Below] By 1931, the fleet of Regals operated by Blue Belle Motors Ltd had expanded to the point that this scene was recorded by the camera at the company's 'London Terminal Coach Station' at 82 Clapham Road, in south-west London [itself remarkable, having been claimed as the first coach station designed and built as such in London when opened in 1929]. An initial order for 30 Regals in 1930 had been followed up by repeat orders. All but one of the coaches visible is positively identifiable as a Regal — the Blue Belle fleet was entirely of this make, apart from some Commer 20-seaters.

Queen Line was another concern involved in operating coaches in the London area and its Kings Cross-Baldock service was another business taken over by Green Line, in this case in April 1933. The six vehicles taken over, all dating from 1931 and having London Lorries bodywork, were all shown in AEC records as having chassis numbered between 662601 and 630 that had been originally ordered by Blue Belle Motors. The vehicle seen here at AEC's Southall works bears no registration number but the body design is a subtly modernised variant of the 1930 London Lorries style, not quite so low-built and with a more upright windscreen reducing the peaked-cap effect of the front canopy. The ex-Queen Line vehicles taken over by Green Line were numbered T352-357, becoming London Transport Country buses with new Weymann bodywork in 1935 but were sent to Germany to operate for the Control Commission in 1945 and never returned. Note that the front hub cap design has again changed to what was to remain its final form for 662-series chassis.

The largest Regal user during the 1930-31 period was the Green Line organisation, though the first steps in this direction were not made under that name. The London General Omnibus Co began operation of an express coach service between Golders Green and Watford in the latter part of 1929. It was soon decided to introduce a body design specifically intended for this type of express duty and one of the 50 Regal chassis ordered as LGOC buses was diverted as a basis. T38, on chassis 662065, thus received a 28-seat rear-entrance body unlike those of any of its direct predecessors. Built at LGOC's Chiswick works, it was noticeably taller than other single-deckers of the period, with generous internal headroom and a high waistline. The 'architecture' was otherwise quite like that of the contemporary Regal buses, but the cab front was of the new rounded style. It entered service in LGOC red livery on the Golders Green-Watford service in January 1930 and remained there for most if not all of its career, being seen here at Golders Green in the mid-'thirties, by then in green livery. It was sold for scrap in March 1939.

The style of bodywork favoured by LGOC for its coaches in the late 'twenties was repeated on five Regals purchased for private hire duties and placed in service in April-May 1930. In terms of chassis and registration numbers, these vehicles came before the first bulk order for coaches, but they were allocated the fleet numbers after them, thus being T150-154. The canvas-roofed bodywork was built by Hoyal and seating was provided for 32 passengers. The style was in the low-loading idiom much favoured at the time, quite unlike the Green Line vehicles proper, though they were painted in Green Line livery in London Transport days, as shown here. Fleet numbers had not been used for these vehicles in the 1931-33 period and when they were revived, they were applied in registration number order, GF 479 became T150 as seen here, though it had orginally been T154, chassis 662216. The batch was sold in 1938, though some reappeared with other operators.

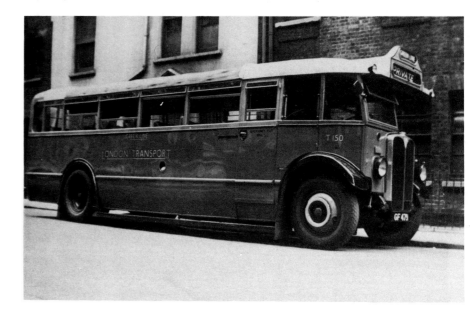

The production vehicles derived from T38 also began to appear in April 1930, though these early vehicles were still not at first Green Line coaches, appearing in the liveries of LGOC or its subsidiaries, Autocar or East Surrey. Green Lines Coaches Ltd was formed in July 1930 and T122 was one of the first to appear in green livery, though seen here in the slightly different style adopted after London Transport had been formed. Soon the whole batch, [chassis numbers 662353-451], T51-149, all became Green Line coaches and are generally referred to as such. A further vehicle, T155 [662299], had actually been the development vehicle making up the initial 100, and a further 50 were numbered T157-206 [662503-552]. All these had 27-seat rear-entrance bodywork derived from that on T38, but with more rounded styling at the rear. Construction was shared equally by LGOC, Short Bros and Hall, Lewis. When London Transport introduced its classification system in 1935, they were coded 7T7. Many, including T122, were sold in 1938-39 and quite a few saw long periods of further service with other operators.

Expansion of the Green Line fleet was impressively rapid. Hardly were the last of the 150 rear-entrance Regals in service in October 1930 before the first examples of a further 100 began to appear in December of that year. All but three had the newly-introduced 110 mm-bore petrol engines. Bodywork, though similar in its characteristic overall appearance to the previous batch, was now of 30-seat front-entrance type and the Green Line illuminated panel at the front was now carried below rather than above the destination indicator — there was plenty of room for it there without restricting the driver's forward vision because of the tall build of the bodywork. This time the body contracts were split between Weymann [25 vehicles], Ransomes [25] and Duple [50]. The standard coding was 1/7T7/1. The batch were numbered T207-306, the chassis allocated being 662703-802 in order, although in practice 662716 was diverted for use by East Surrey and another chassis, 662803, was built for T220. The vehicle shown, T251, is seen in the original style of livery with broad black waistband, at the Victoria stopping point.

Chapter Three : A choice of power

At first, the Regal had been sold with a relatively standardised specification, although operators' preferences in such matters as make of electrical equipment or carburettor were often indulged. Gradually, however, a wider choice was offered. The original engine design had allowed for a larger swept volume of 7.4-litres by increasing the bore size to 110 mm. By using this in conjunction with a higher geared rear axle, a top speed of 60 mph was possible, and among early examples were four coaches supplied in May 1930 for the Newcastle-London service operated by Orange Bros, in those days an independent concern based at Bedlington. The fleet of 100 coaches for Green Line service delivered early in 1931 (T207-306) were also of this specification, apart from a few special exceptions. By about the end of 1931, the larger engine had become usual and the 100 mm unit faded out of production.

Not everyone wanted more power, and in June 1930 it was decided to convert a stock Regal chassis, 662277, replacing its 110 mm bore engine (possibly one of the first) with a four-cylinder 5.1-litre unit of the type also of overhead-camshaft Rackham design that was being used in the contemporary Mercury and Monarch goods chassis — in fact the engine came from one. Thus was born the Regal 4 and in fact in August 1930, the chassis was renumbered 642001, thus becoming the first of this type. Its Middlesex registration number HX 1271, suggests that it saw a period of demonstration service presumably in this form before being restored

to original six-cylinder form and regaining the chassis number 662277 and being sold to Bell's Services Ltd of Westerhope near Newcastle, later passing into the United Automobile Services fleet.

A handful of sales of Regal 4 models followed, though the second vehicle was again a conversion from a standard Regal 662480 which became 642002 and was sold in this form to Stockton Corporation as UP 4744. Sales of this model picked up slightly after 1932, but never rivalled those of the competitive Leyland Lion or Dennis Lancet models.

A more significant engine option was the oil engine announced by AEC in October 1930. Most of the early examples were fitted to double-decker chassis, and it seems probable that the first Regals so equipped may have been Green Line coaches T216, 274 and 305 (chassis numbers 662712, 770 and 801) although SMT's SC 9871 (662839) first registered in March 1931 is another contender. These early indirect injection oil engines were 8.1-litre six-cylinder units developing 95 bhp and incorporated Acro combustion chambers. Like the 8.8-litre unit with Ricardo cylinder head developed from them, they were about 4½in. longer than the six-cylinder petrol engine and had the radiator set forward by this distance.

Some trouble was experienced with these early Acro oil engines and both operators and AEC itself tended to proceed rather warily for a year or two. The AEC-Ricardo unit became a thoroughly reliable unit, if not quite the equal of the best direct-injection

units in terms of fuel consumption, but its extra length, which meant a corresponding cut in the space available for passengers was a drawback, particularly on a single-decker. The overall length limit for a two-axle single-decker had been standardised at 27ft. 6in. from 1931 and the Regal's wheelbase was correspondingly increased to 17ft. 6in. from the following year — remaining so on home market models up to 1950. Even so, the oil-engined AEC gave virtually no gain in passenger space as a result of the extra length and this factor did not help sales.

There was, in any case, only very limited interest in diesel engines for coaches at that time, and even among buses, few company fleets were yet prepared to changeover from petrol — AEC's extra chassis price of some £300, enough to buy a good medium-sized car, was also a deterrent. Most other manufacturers of competitive vehicles were offering six-cylinder petrol engines and the AEC's lead in front-end layout, and appearance had largely vanished — in mid-1933, Leyland's new TS6 version of the Tiger looked if anything even more modern, as well as accommodating, if required, an 8.6-litre oil engine within a bonnet length an inch shorter than the Regal's.

The Gilford challenge had begun to fade even before the takeover of many of that firm's customers by London Transport. Daimler, whose CF6 model based on the ADC 423 but with a larger 5.7-litre version of the sleeve-valve engine had done well in 1929-30, was for the time being no longer a major challenger for single-decker

The Regal's front-end design altered only slightly during the model's first eight years, a remarkable survival during a period of rapid change, though it was Rackham's classic design which largely set the pace for the remainder. This was the 1931 version, with re-arranged bonnet louvres and access holes in the bonnet side to allow checking and replenishment of engine oil, the latter being a new feature that was to remain characteristic of most AEC models until 1947 and was widely copied by other manufacturers. It had become standard practice to provide both dash panels at both front and rear of the bonnet, these being very square cut as shown, although the edges could be trimmed to some extent by bodybuilders. The triangulated support bracket for the front dash was intended only for delivery; the panel and entire cab structure were to be supported by the body, adequate clearance being provided around the radiator to allow for relative movement which could easily be seen from within the vehicle.

business. Dennis, however, had made a major come-back with the mechanically simple four-cylinder Lancet with its excellent value for a chassis price of £595, while Bristol was about to begin taking an increasing share of company business as a result of its newly-established position in the Tilling group, displacing Tilling-Stevens from that position after a brief interval.

The 1932 six-cylinder Regal was by no means cheap at £1,050 in its least expensive form (even though this was slightly less than the £1,100 charged in the 1929-31 period), but its specification had been improved. The 110 mm bore engine had, from the 1932 season, been modified

to give 120 bhp with a 'high-power' cylinder head with improved gas flow, making this the most powerful petrol engine available in a British bus chassis at the time apart from the somewhat exotic Sunbeam. On paper, there was little opportunity to use such high performance for although the speed limit for buses and coaches had been raised to 30 mph, the scheduled point-to-point speeds on express services were now often limited to 22 mph. In practice, speed still had its appeal.

The Regal was also available with vacuum-hydraulic brakes at first available as an extra cost option but later standard. There had already been an intermediate improvement in

design when a so-called 'three-servo' system replaced the single servo in 1931.

The standard four-speed gearbox had been improved by 1931, incorporating a constant-mesh third gear to give easier changes into that ratio, but the contemporary literature's refference to a "silent third" was no more than wishful thinking, as the straight-cut gear teeth remained unchanged and the characteristic AEC gear whine was to continue until the early 'fifties.

A more important transmission development was the introduction in 1932 as an option of Daimler fluid flywheel transmission, at first incorporating Daimler-built preselective gearboxes. Lord Ashfield had realised the potential value of this development, no doubt with the heavy wear and tear on conventional transmission of bus operation in London mainly in mind, but the agreement to supply AEC with sets of Daimler-built units covered sale to any operator. AEC publicity encouraged operators to adopt this feature at an extra cost of £100 and although double-deckers on urban service were the most obvious application, quite a few orders were placed for fluid transmission Regals, generally with petrol engines for the first couple of years or so. Early operators of such Regals included Leeds, Huddersfield and Colne Corporations and Thomas Tilling, the last-mentioned order referring to the first two of a dozen examples which were also noteworthy for having a small-bore (95 mm) version of the standard AEC petrol engine, giving a swept volume of only 5½ litres. They were numbered T307-318 in the LGOC series. A few coach operators also chose fluid flywheel transmission, although the standard crash gearbox remained much the more popular choice.

Noteworthy among company orders in 1932 was one from SMT for 60 Regals. As built, these had petrol engines and Alexander rear-entrance bus bodywork but the SMT group's interest in diesel engines was to be confirmed by an order for six Regal coaches with the 8.8-litre unit and fluid transmission for the London service supplied in 1933 and a dozen more in 1934, and later to be the subject of rebuilding as double-deckers during the war period.

Among the last chassis to be supplied having the 1930 type of front hub cap was 662975 placed in service by the Amersham & District Bus & Haulage Co Ltd in April 1931; such variations in specification were by no means related to the numerical order of chassis. This concern tended to base its choice of vehicles, livery and fleetname style [with the reference to haulage deleted] on that of the Aldershot & District Traction Co Ltd, despite having no relationship to that concern. Dennis chassis and Strachans bodywork tended to be favoured in true Aldershot fashion, but from 1930, the Amersham company began a period of co-operation with the LGOC and its Green Line subsidiary — in January 1931, four of the 1930 batch of Green Line Regals had been transferred to Amersham & District to work an express service to Oxford Circus in central London. The vehicle shown was the first of six Regals with Strachans 32-seat rear-entrance coach bodywork to be supplied new to the company, though two Regents were delivered in 1930. The entire fleet was taken over by London Transport in November 1933, KX 6785 becoming T364. The vehicle must rank as among the most elegant Regals in the idiom of its time — the dark green and cream livery was in a style that had been favoured by the Aldershot company prior to 1929.

The Regal's export potential was realised from the beginning. In some markets, notably South America, AEC vehicles were sold under the ACLO make name to meet an embargo on the use of AEC that had been won by the German electrical concern, AEG. Hence this was strictly speaking an ACLO Regal which was being inspected by none other than the Prince of Wales during a tour of that continent in 1931 — he can be identified by the straw hat worn at a jaunty angle. The vehicle had close resemblances to contemporary LGOC practice in body design, but had its entrance on the right to suit the rule of the road as well as full-drop opening windows.

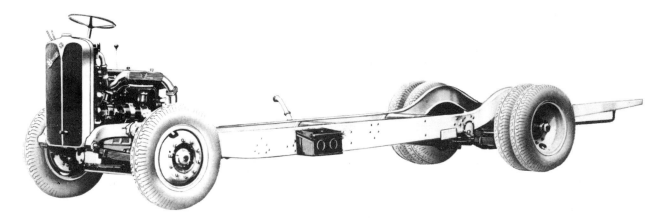

[Above] Both the first two Regal 4 chassis to be produced were conversions from six-cylinder models. On the print from which this picture was made, it is possible to see a number which seems to have been chalked alongside the left-hand front dumb-iron, possibly reading 642002. If so, this is the chassis sold to Stockton Corporation in 1930, the second built but the first four-cylinder Regal to find a buyer — it was registered UP 4744 and had Brush 32-seat bodywork, remaining until sold to Brown of Tunstall which whom it was observed in 1943. Note the shorter engine and the 1930-style front hub. The model was hardly a runaway success, with the total built still in single figures after the first year or so.

[Below] By contrast, an almost certain candidate for the new more powerful 110 mm-bore six-cylinder engine was 662883, the last of four chassis supplied via Tillotsons to Majestic Saloon Coaches [Newcastle and London] Ltd of Ebchester, Co. Durham in April-May 1931. Burlingham built the 26-seat bodywork, space at the rear being provided for luggage accommodation. A noteworthy detail was the provision of a 'Majestic' script title on the radiator of the type used on the contemporary AEC goods model of that name, the normal 'Regal' title being moved to a lower position on the nearside of the radiator. United Automobile Services Ltd, by then based in Darlington, acquired the Majestic long-distance coach business in August 1932, although it was at first continued as a separate subsidiary, and this vehicle remained in service, latterly as a bus but not greatly altered in appearance, until about 1950.

In a time of rapid changes of vehicle design, it was all too easy to be caught out with dating appearance on a new vehicle. In this 1931 scene, possibly photographed in the premises of The Birmingham Garages Ltd, AEC's distributors in that city, Red Warrior's new Regal OG 9085, evidently ready for delivery, has more the look of a 1929-30 vehicle — the half-canopy cab had temporarily gone out of general favour. Alongside is Birmingham City Tramways and Omnibus Department's No. 388, a Regent with body to characteristic style built by English Electric delivered the previous year, apparently in for repair, no doubt because it was still under warranty — engine removal was relatively simple on such vehicles.

[Above] Aircraft design has changed even more dramatically than coach design over the period of a little over half a century since this picture was taken at Croydon Airport in 1931, then the principal airport serving London. The aircraft was one of the Handley-Page HP42 38-seat four-engined biplanes then used on the London-Paris service. The AEC Regal, GO 1381, was leased by Thomas Tilling Ltd to Imperial Airways whose name it carried. Bodywork was by Harrington — the oval rear window was for a while characteristic of this bodybuilder.

[Below] The Rhondda Valley in South Wales provided a contrasting type of background for Regal 6621126, one of ten Regals supplied to the Rhondda Tramways Co Ltd in 1931, the vehicle shown, No. 82, being the first of nine with Weymann bodywork, the beginning of a long run of Weymann-bodied vehicles for this operator, generally on AEC chassis. Earlier in the year, six Bristol D-type single-deckers had been purchased and one of these can be seen following — the D-type was typical of numerous six-cylinder models introduced by various makers to compete with the Leyland Tiger and AEC Regal. Rhondda Tramways had tended to split its orders between AEC and Bristol, but from this period, AEC predominated, with a minority of Dennis until 1937 — the company became a BET subsidiary in 1932 and changed its title to Rhondda Transport on the abandonment of trams in 1934.

Hull, or to use its full title, Kingston-upon-Hull Corporation received a big intake of new buses in 1932-33, mainly double-deckers for tram replacement. Among the first to arrive, however, were ten Regals of which 6621192, numbered 7 in the fleet is seen here. It had bodywork by the English Electric Co Ltd, originally seating 28 with two door-ways, later altered to 31-seat capacity with a rear-entrance only. It survived in service until 1949. Note the general lack of traffic, apart from bicycles, despite the number of people about.

Furey's Tours was an enterprising tour operator in Dublin, for whom this Strachans-bodied coach was built towards the end of 1931. Three Regals from this fleet, almost certainly including the vehicle shown, were taken over by the Great Southern Railway in 1935, passing to CIE in 1945 although withdrawn almost immediately.

There was appreciable interest in the use of passenger chassis for special-purpose goods bodywork in the early 'thirties, generally exploiting the low-loading possibilities. Among AEC examples was this display van built in 1932 for the Ardath tobacco concern to display the goods obtainable in exchange for coupons. The bodywork was built by Strachans and incorporated a combination of goods and passenger vehicle characteristics. Later a specific model, the original Mandator, was introduced to cater for this market, retaining the passenger chassis profile but with goods vehicle equipment.

By 1932, a further subtle change was occurring in coach body styling. Overall height had generally settled down somewhere between the ultra-low level of many early Regal designs and the taller vehicles built by some concerns. Thus Harrington's new standard coach style, one of the most attractive of its era, was slightly lower-built than its predecessors, but had the more rounded roof line which was another feature on which there was general agreement, in this case with built-in side display panel. More thought was being given to detail design such as the windscreen and front window outlines and the moulded waistline, in this case emphasised by continuing the colour band along the edge of the bonnet top, was a typical feature. Just visible through the interior in the above view, taken in the AEC photographer's favourite location at Southall works, are the curved glass rear corner windows, an early attempt at all-round vision. The vehicle was for H. A. Roberts of Norwich, later Red Car Services [Norwich] Ltd, which continued in business until recent times.

Another Harrington customer was W. Salisbury & Sons Ltd of Blackpool, evidently preferring, on this occasion, to 'import' coach bodywork from the south rather than patronise the local Burlingham concern. This pair of vehicles shown below, FV 2896 and 2920, photographed in Autumn 1932, had a basically similar body design to that illustrated above but the appearance was further modernised by eliminating the last remnant of the running board and incorporating the operator's illuminated name sign within the roof line at the front. The Salisbury concern later came into the Ribble empire, its vehicles being absorbed into the Standerwick coach-operating subsidiary.

Despite quite encouraging overall sales in a period when several competitive manufacturers were struggling, orders for Regals for the major regional bus operating companies were at first rather limited, rarely exceeding quantities of ten or a dozen, to a fairly modest number of such operators. The Scottish Motor Traction Co Ltd had similarly started fairly cautiously after purchasing a 1930 demonstrator and, in 1931, an early oil-engined example, by placing eleven coaches with 110 mm petrol engines in service in 1931. However, for 1932 an order for some 60 Regals was placed, at once making SMT the largest Regal user outside London. The body order went to W. Alexander & Sons Ltd, which, with its newly opened works in Stirling, was just beginning its role as principal bodybuilder to the then SMT group as well as being the largest

bus operating concern in the group. The 1932 Regal bodies were 32-seat buses of the cutaway rear-entrance design which continued to be favoured by SMT for its own buses through most of the 'thirties. The chassis were supplied in two batches, 6621201-40 and 1260-79, but were numbered B14-72 and registered FS 2251-2309, though not in chassis number order. They were to prove exceptionally long-lived, albeit re-engined with 7.7-litre oil engines and rebodied, the entire batch [apart from a 1934 accident casualty] surviving until 1957-59, mostly thus remaining in service upwards of 25 years. B62 is seen here when quite new, showing the purposeful and distinctive appearance of the original bodywork.

Independent operators were still playing a major part in long-distance express service operation in the early 'thirties, even though the 1930 Road Traffic Act produced a climate which encouraged purchase of such business by the larger groups. This Regal was supplied to Tyne & Mersey Motor Services Ltd whose address is quoted on the vehicle as 6 Haymarket, Newcastle-upon-Tyne, which was alongside the bus station used as a terminal for most long-distance services. The photograph was taken on a dismal early summer day in 1932 at the substantial premises of Oswald Tillotson Ltd in Burnley. Bodywork in this case was by Duple, again to a style very much in the idiom of the times — note the panel used to hide the Autovac fuel lift alongside the bonnet.

[Above] Huddersfield Corporation was by 1932 a regular AEC customer. This line-up at Nont Sarah's includes one each of oil-engined [ie diesel] and petrol versions of the Regal and a couple of petrol Regents, all with Northern Counties bodywork and supplied that year. The leading vehicle, No. 150 [chassis number 6621372] had the oil engine and in addition to the script on the radiator informing onlookers of the fact, its projecting radiator threw a deeper shadow than on petrol-engined No. 151 immediately behind — also it lacked a starting handle, hand starting doubtless being considered impractical with the 8.8-litre engine. Though still uncommon, the AEC oil engine was beginning to be used in an appreciable proportion of the maker's vehicles. Four Regals of this batch of ten, possibly including No. 151, and three out of six of the Regents had fluid flywheel transmission.

[Below] Many of the smaller coach operators were placing repeat orders for Regals. H. W. Pilcher of Chatham was able to line up this display, the three leading vehicles dating respectively from 1932, 1931 and 1930. This operator favoured the use of polished aluminium for bonnet top and side panels, and in this view the variations of louvre arrangement on these three vehicles can be seen. The latest, newly in service when photographed in the early summer of 1932, had two rows of vertical louvres, a design introduced at about that time. The petrol engine could run rather hot in adverse conditions and the new style was doubtless an attempt to mitigate overheating. A more major change introduced at that time was the alteration of wheelbase to 17ft. 6in. to suit the increase in maximum length to 27ft. 6in.

Another Yorkshire municipality to specify the new fluid transmission option was Leeds City Tramways and Transport Department. Six petrol Regals delivered in 1932 were so fitted, 6621383, Leeds No. 30, being shown here. Weymann built the 32-seat rear-entrance bodywork, typical of the builder's products of the period. One senses a certain nervousness as to whether a fluid flywheel and Wilson-type preselective epicyclic gearbox would prove adequate as a city bus transmission, as only one of eleven Regents for Leeds was similarly equipped and, in London, Thomas Tilling chose two Regals for similar transmission experience. However, Leeds was soon won over and Regents with oil engines and fluid transmission were standard from 1934, though no further Regals were bought. These early installations incorporated units supplied by Daimler. The Leeds livery at that date was an attractive light blue with cream waistline, introduced by the recently-appointed General Manager, W. Vane Morland — he had favoured a similar livery in his previous appointment at Walsall.

Burlingham's standard coach design was another which, though related to its predecessors of 1932-32 was subtly changing. This example, for John Eccles of Chestergate, Macclesfield, registered ALG 75, was completed late in 1932. In addition to slightly higher build than hitherto favoured by Burlingham, the shaped pillars with decorative emblem were to be characteristic of this maker for a couple of seasons. Note that three-letter registration marks had now appeared for the first time in a few areas.

The observation coach, with rear portion significantly higher than the front, had a brief run of limited popularity in Britain around 1929-30. By 1933 it was generally considered an obsolete concept, but Blue Belle Coaches Ltd revived the idea, ordering ten Regals to be so bodied. This one, AGJ 928, was the first and had bodywork built by J. C. Beadle Ltd of Dartford, Kent. Seats were provided for 35 passengers, a high capacity at that time, as well as generous accommodation for luggage. Though not pursued further at that date, the idea was the basis of many later airport coaches.

Keen competition was fostering fresh ideas in coach design and this Duple body on petrol Regal chassis for Corona Coaches of Sudbury, Suffolk was remarkably modern-looking for early 1933. The centre entrance had been favoured by some municipal operators since the 'twenties but was uncommon on a coach. The revival of the half-canopy front end, out of favour for a few years, was a pointer to later standard practice though unusual at that period. The key feature which was soon to be standard but was a novelty at the time was the outswept skirt.

Individual bodybuilders were often each willing to produce a bewildering variety of styles and there can hardly have been a major item in common between this Duple style and that shown above, save perhaps the windscreen. This design was quite popular briefly in 1932-33 but its turned-under rear skirt and other details were already beginning to become outmoded. The example shown was supplied to James Sutherland of Peterhead early in 1933.

[Below] Short Bros of Rochester were major bus bodybuilders until 1935 but briefly entered the coach market with this style in 1933. An advertisement in June of that year claimed that its elimination of the conventional waistband was a step forward in design — in fact the continuous waistband was to go out of favour but was replaced by other forms of decoration. AGJ 614 and 615 [6621483-4] were supplied to Julius & Lockwood of Lewisham, London SE.

[Above] The British Electric Traction group had an offshoot, British Electrical Federation Ltd, which provided services for BET operating companies and, among other items, supervised vehicle specifications. Some companies standardised on Federation body designs, but not many of these were regular AEC customers. So bodywork of the style shown was more often found on Leyland Tiger or Lion chassis than on a Regal. The South Wales Transport Co Ltd had been an AEC user in the 'twenties but had largely favoured Dennis vehicles in the 1928-32 period. No. 301 [WN 5401], on chassis 6621490, was the first of ten petrol Regals with what were described as luxury saloon bodywork with seats for 28 passengers and built by Weymann. Unusually for this type of body, a flush-fitting outward opening entrance door was fitted, a feature which, like the body design as a whole, was rather dated for a coach built in 1933. The batch was impressed for use by the Royal Air Force in July 1940 and this vehicle was one of six lost due to enemy action.

[Below] Another, very different, Regal for an operator in South Wales was this one for Enterprize Motor Service [Gorseinon] Ltd. It was oil-engined, having the 8.8-litre unit which was at that date the only such unit available in the 662-type Regal chassis. Short Bros built the body-work — the cutaway rear entrance had a following in Wales as well as Scotland at that date. Enterprize merged with D. Bassett & Sons [Gorse-inon] Ltd in 1935 to form Bassett-Enterprise Ltd and in 1938 was involved in a larger merger with other Swansea area subsidiaries of J. H. Watts' Red & White empire to form United Welsh Services Ltd. This photo-graph conveys the markedly different appearance given by the 8.8-litre engine with the radiator mounted further forward, slightly inclined and a little higher than on the petrol-engined version.

A. Timpson & Sons Ltd regularly added batches of Harrington-bodied Regals to its fleet in the early 'thirties. The company was still operating a branch in Hastings when the 1933 vehicles arrived and so they received DY registration numbers, although the Catford-based business in London was far more important and the Hastings branch was sold with the local bus business later that year. Three of them can be seen at the front of this scene, taken in the summer of 1937 when about 20 Regals were used for the staff outing of CAV Ltd, the electrical and fuel-injection equipment maker, from its Acton works; Timpson's specialised in such work. The 1933 Harrington half-canopy design was another trend-setter, though perhaps more as a prototype for some mid-'thirties bus development, as coaches were soon to become distinctly more exotic. Even so, these Timpson's vehicles continued to look very smart in their cream and chocolate livery, some continuing well into the post-war period, including 6621467, the leading vehicle shown.

A change in specification for the Regal which became evident during 1933 was the changeover from the semi-floating type of rear axle to the fully-floating type, with consequent replacement of the relatively small octagonal rear hub with a larger unit. The alteration had been made after reports of isolated rear axle shaft failures, and followed a similar change in the Leyland range at the end of 1931. In AEC's case, it was not associated with a specific change of model and the later axle could readily be fitted to earlier chassis, though this was by no means common even when vehicles were extensively modernised; the failures were evidently rare. An early example of the later design was this Strachans-bodied vehicle for Keith Coaches [Mills & Adams] of Aylesbury, Bucks. Although not identified, it may have been ABH 307 which was 6621519.

Although the numbers of Regals sold were not as high in 1932-33 as they had been in 1931, the model was still one of the most popular in its class and probably received a greater variety of body styles — there being no standard version — than any other type. Duple alone built numerous body designs on Regal chassis, in some cases never to be exactly repeated, though 6621521 [ALM 266] built in the summer of 1933 for the Sceptre Coaches fleet of Bingley Bros of Hammersmith, was almost identical to a coach built for the Eastern Belle fleet of which the interior — typical of a Regal coach of the period — is seen below. Travel in such a vehicle was comparable to that in a contemporary luxury car, with the smooth petrol engine almost inaudible when idling.

Sales of the Regal 4 improved a little in 1933. This petrol-engined example for Fraser Bros of Lantran, Inverness, is seen when new about to set off from AEC's Southall works in the hands of its owners on its 500-mile journey north. No. 11 had bodywork by Park Royal and evidently gave satisfaction, for another Regal 4 was purchased the following year though with oil engine and locally-built Walker bodywork [See Best of British No. 3, page 57]. Both vehicles were taken over with the Fraser business by the Highland Transport Co Ltd in 1939, the later one surviving long enough to be transferred again to Highland Omnibuses Ltd on its formation in 1951 and not being withdrawn until 1953.

Chapter Four : Mid 'thirties variety

Total sales of Regal models had slowed down quite markedly in 1932 and 1933, amounting to around 500, about half of those of the first two years of production and although this was partly the result of the general depression in trade, which seemed to affect the bus and coach business slightly later than some other industries, it no doubt helped to foster new developments at Southall. In some ways, sales were a victim of previous success. With a complete new Green Line coach fleet and single-deck bus fleet supplied in 1929-31, London had no requirement for new Regals. Some sales activity was doubtless being diverted to the side-engined Q type (see 'Best of British Buses No. 2'), though with no more than limited success.

A new four-cylinder oil engine of 5.35-litres capacity was introduced in March 1933 and later in the year a Regal 4 was used to demonstrate its capabilities to operators. Later the swept volume was increased to 6.6-litres and this unit did help to improve sales of the model, although there had also been a modest rise in numbers of the petrol version built in 1933, with orders for about half-a-dozen

vehicles each from such concerns as the City of Oxford, East Midland and Mansfield District companies. Even so, with total sales since 1930 of not much over 50 vehicles it was hardly a roaring success.

However, in 1934 there was a distinct upturn, with about 80 Regal 4 sold that year, largely on the basis of the oil-engined model. Dublin United Transport Co Ltd had taken delivery of one example in 1933, put 25 more into service in 1934, and brought its total fleet up to 46 with a final 20 in 1935. This was to prove the largest Regal 4 fleet, though SMT took 33 in one order, again with oil engines, in 1934. Perhaps the best-known Regal 4 models of all, however, were the eight supplied to the Gosport and Fareham (Provincial) fleet, again in 1934, all of which survived, albeit much rebuilt and with six-cylinder engines from 1945-46, until 1966-70.

Only about 100 of the standard six-cylinder Regal were sold in 1934, with the powerful, but bulky and somewhat thirsty 8.8-litre A165 Ricardo-head engine appealing mainly to municipalities in hilly districts — Halifax and Sheffield — apart from the SMT coaches already mentioned

and a few other coach operators plus small numbers for BET fleets. Coaches accounted for most of the petrol examples, apart from a dozen with fluid transmission for Huddersfield.

However, in 1935 the standard oil engine for the six-cylinder Regal switched to the A171 so-called 7.7-litre (actually 7.58-litre) unit that was derived from the oil engine developed for the Q type. This fitted into the standard Regal bonnet and yet in original Ricardo indirect-injection form gave 115 bhp, ample for a 27ft. 6in. long single-decker. SMT, becoming established as the most regular major Regal customer, placed 39 examples in service in the summer of 1935, split between 25 Alexander-bodied coaches and fourteen Cowieson buses, and other orders began to come in from a variety of operators.

Despite this promising 'mainstream' development, work was in hand on yet another new Regal variant. Introduced as the Regal Mark II at the 1935 Commercial Motor Show, it may well have been hoped that it would eventually supersede the standard Regal. Publicised as a lightweight model, it had a chassis weight modestly reduced by about half a ton.

Though sales of Regals with the 8.8-litre oil engine were never numerous, there was a brief period in 1933 when a few of the more prominent coach operators were persuaded to take delivery of examples. George Ewer & Co Ltd, proprietors of the London-based Grey-Green coach fleet, largely standardised on the Leyland Tiger in the late 'thirties but this oil-engined Regal was one of a few placed in service in 1933-34. Grey-Green was a regular Harrington customer, this vehicle having a version of the standard body design from that concern of the period. The provision of two passenger doors, common in the late 'twenties, had become rare by that date and it was particularly unusual to find sliding doors [by then the accepted type found on coaches] at both front and rear. It is seen at Ewer's Stamford Hill headquarters, comparatively new at the time.

It had a new compact six-cylinder engine of nominally 6.6-litres capacity (actually 6.75-litres, but AEC had become addicted to engine sizes in multiples of 1.1-litres for publicity purposes) available in either oil or petrol versions, the chassis model number being either O862 or 'plain' 862 accordingly, the standard Regal also having an 'O' prefix for oil-engined versions, thus becoming O662, since about 1933. The A172 oil engine was similar in principle to previous AEC indirect-injection engines but having crankcase and cylinder block in one casting, with 'wet' cylinder liners in direct contact with the cooling water.

No doubt the aim was to cut manufacturing cost as well as weight — the chassis price of an O862 was £1,145, compared to £1,250 for the O662 (though the latter was £100 less than had applied in the earlier 'thirties). The remainder of the chassis was largely unchanged —

in fact the prototype was rebuilt from an O662 model — although the appearance was altered by the introduction of a smaller chromium-plated radiator and modified front mudguards.

The new model got off to a good start with an order for 25 built in 1936 for the Northern General Transport Co Ltd (O862003-27), but this was to prove the only single order for more than a dozen — only 104 examples were built, production ending in 1939. Among the most interesting were eight with Daimler preselective gearboxes for South Wales Transport Co Ltd in 1936 — by that date AEC had been in production with its own preselective box for two years, though it was not offered on the Regal Mark II. The wet-liner oil engine is reputed to have been troublesome and it is significant that almost all the later examples were petrol, the largest user being the Ribble coaching subsidiary, Standerwick.

The Regal 4 had also slipped from favour once more, as after the final Dublin United order had been completed in 1935, only about fifteen further examples were built, including notably two for the Burnley, Colne and Nelson Joint Committee in 1936 and the last three for Swindon Corporation in 1937, in both cases with oil engines. The total built since the introduction of the model in 1930 was 177, which must have seemed a disappointing total for a model that was directly comparable to the highly successful Leyland Lion models of the same period, though no attempt had been made to match the latter's more compact front-end as introduced on the LT5A model in 1934. However, the days of the four-cylinder single-decker had virtually come to an end so far as big fleets were concerned, though Dennis was still doing well among independent operators with the Lancet II.

[Above] Another purchaser of an 8.8-litre oil-engined Regal in 1933 was Keith & Boyle [London] Ltd, proprietors of the Orange Luxury Coach, fleet though this vehicle was allocated to the Shamrock & Rambler fleet which in those days was its subsidiary in Bournemouth, sharing the same orange and cream livery for its vehicles. The bodywork was by Weymann, to a design clearly intended to be 'modern', though retaining the traditional type of outward-opening hinged entrance door. The stepped waistrail was a feature that was about to catch on but the unusual treatment of the waist at the front simply remained 'odd'. Overall the styling execution of this interesting design was rather heavy-handed, in the way so often found when a bus bodybuilder attempted a coach styling exercise — note that the cab treatment was very like that of Weymann double-deckers of the period. The vehicle later passed to North Manchester Motors where it was given a new Burlingham coach body in 1949, still retaining the 8.8-litre engine. Note the style of seating, very like that in the special excursion stock built for the London & North Eastern Railway later in the 'thirties.

[Below] An altogether more stylish design was this Harrington coach body for another major London operator, United Service Transport Co Ltd. Believed to have been an exhibit at the November 1933 Commercial Motor Show at Olympia, London, it was of a design which was to set the direction for trends in the appearance of coaches during the next few years. It, too, had a stepped waistline but the seating was ramped, so that each row was slightly higher than that in front. This was a revival of a very old idea found on some open-sided vehicles of the Edwardian era, but its combination with modern external design was novel. Sloping pillars had appeared on a Duple coach on the side-engined AEC Q chassis in August 1933 [see Best of British Buses No. 2, page 32] but their combination here with the stepped waistline and the generous use of graceful curves gave a harmonious look to the vehicle as a whole. Harrington had a styling winner and similar designs — though perhaps not quite retaining the flair of the 1934 season original — were to come out of the Hove works throughout the 'thirties.

It was easy to slip out of step with styling trends and Burlingham, among the leaders of thinking in 1931-32, seemed to slip a little around 1934 when some rather fussy designs with short window bays were produced. This one, on chassis 6621540, for Wilson Bros of Whitehaven, was fairly typical — it was acquired with the Wilson business by Cumberland Motor Services Ltd in 1936.

J. C. Beadle Ltd of Dartford produced this interesting design on a Regal for W. Salisbury & Sons Ltd of Blackpool. The four-bay layout may have been inspired by Leyland's design as introduced on the TS6 chassis early in 1933 [see Best of British Buses No. 3, pages 32-33], but the front end detail work, with an almost exaggerated downward sweep to the windscreen and 'scalloped' front canopy, had echoes of earlier Beadle styles.

Charles Rickards Ltd of Paddington often tended to be in the limelight because of its involvement in official occasions in London as holder of the Royal Warrant. However, these two 1934 Regals in the restrained maroon livery were conveying schoolchildren when photographed in Whitehall, passing the Cenotaph on a wet spring day in 1939. Note the 1937-model Austin saloon.

[Above] Isle of Man Road Services Ltd took delivery of one oil-engined Regal 4, 642059, numbered 51 in its fleet and registered MN 5108, in 1934, seen here in service the following year. The Burlingham bus body seated 34. At the same date IOMRS took delivery of five Leyland Lion LT5A models and subsequent orders also went to Leyland.

[Below] This Regal 4 oil-engined demonstrator was painted in Maidstone & District dark green livery in the latter part of 1934. The unprepossessing bodywork appears somewhat dated and might have been of earlier origin. No order from M & D materialised from the exercise, though this operator was to become a major user of six-cylinder Regals in the post-1945 era. The picture, shows the characteristic broad sump of the four-cylinder oil engine, clearly visible behind the registration plate. The engine oil filler also differed from the six-cylinder petrol [or later 7.7-litre oil] version, being slightly higher and less inclined. Note that the radiator, surprisingly, was mounted slightly further forward than with either the four or six-cylinder petrol engine, though not as much so as with the 8.8-litre six-cylinder oil unit — no attempt was made to reduce bonnet length as with the LT5A.

This three-quarter rear view of a typical BET Federation single-decker of the period would, at first glance, probably be taken to be a Leyland Tiger — large numbers of such vehicles were going into service with companies which favoured this style of bodywork up and down the country. But, overleaf, it will be seen .....

..... that the vehicle illustrated at the foot of the previous page was in fact one of eight AEC Regals with 8.8-litre oil engines for the Western Welsh Omnibus Company Ltd. Weymann built the 32-seat bodywork to BET Federation design — although generally to the latter's standard, these vehicles had sliding entrance doors and the illuminated 'double W' symbol carried above the Clayton destination indicator which was itself taller than the remainder of the roof structure. The batch, built early in 1934, had chassis O6621564-71, being registered KG 3605-12. This was another instance where Leyland were to follow, for subsequent orders for Western Welsh single-deckers had similar bodywork on Tiger chassis, though there were to be further AECs, mainly double-deckers, from time to time from 1940 onwards.

The AEC works photographer's next picture was of another Regal with the A165 8.8-litre engine for a BET company. One of six for Northern General Transport Co Ltd, it had bodywork by Short Bros of a style incorporating that builder's standard features of the period and only following BET Federation practice in such items as the severely rectangular Clayton destination indicator and the inset entrance door. Northern was interested in maximum seating capacity, being precluded from operating double-deckers on several of its most intensive routes by bridges, often carrying the industrial railways so characteristic of the Tyneside area. A seating capacity of 36 — about the maximum practicable on an 8.8-litre Regal — was provided by putting the rearmost four rows of seats on raised platforms to allow them to give adequate leg room over the rear wheel arches — single seats faced sideways on each side at the front. No. 600 on chassis O6621584 entered service in April 1934, was rebodied by Pickering in 1946, and was not withdrawn until December 1955, then being exported to Enterprise Bus Service, Jamaica.

[Above] Huddersfield Corporation, though clear in its choice of AEC chassis for all but small buses, was passing through a period of uncertainty about the choice of engines. Despite early experience of the oil-engined Regal, the 1934 order reverted to petrol engines. However, preselective transmission was now accepted as standard. The vehicle shown, No. 6 [VH 6523] on chassis number 6621516, was one of six supplied in 1934 with Park Royal 32-seat bodywork — a further six had very similar bodywork by Brush. These vehicles were sold in 1944-45 and several saw further service with independent operators. The vehicle bears lettering for Huddersfield's joint bus operations with the London Midland and Scottish Railway although in this case owned by the Corporation. The livery at that period was an attractive combination of maroon, red and cream. For some curious reason, this photograph was used in the preliminary publicity concerning the Regal Mark II in Autumn 1935 despite its lack of resemblance to that model.

[Below] Probably the longest-lived of all Regals in terms of continued revenue-earning service were the eight Regal 4 models with Harrington 32-seat bus bodies based on the 1933 coach style placed in service in 1934 by the Gosport and Fareham Omnibus Company. All were still in service up to 1966 and the last was not finally retired until 1970, when 36 years old. All had been re-engined — the original four-cylinder oil engines being replaced by new 7.7-litre units in 1945-46 — and the original bodies were extensively rebuilt between 1948 and 1955, followed by rebodying between 1958 and 1962, as recounted fully in "Provincial - the Gosport and Fareham story", published by TPC. Their appearance was altered drastically [though whether improved is a matter of controversy], but the survival of no more than the chassis was a remarkable indication of the potential longevity of AEC products of the 'thirties.

[Above] On this pair of pages four varieties of Duple coach built within a few months are represented, as well as contemporary Burlingham and Harrington products. The rear-entrance Duple body shown above was another instance of a four-bay design evidently inspired by the pioneer Leyland coach style of 1933 and was perhaps the best-looking of this school of design of the 1933-34 period. The example shown was built for J. R. Street & Son, Hertford in 1934.

[Right] However, tastes were altering and this front-entrance design was produced for James Sutherland of Peterhead towards the end of 1934, the lettering on the windows suggesting that it was displayed at the Scottish Show that year. The front end is almost identical to that of the Street vehicle, but the new curved roof line was a foretaste of later development while the sloping pillars and stepped waistline were in tune with current fashion.

[Below] When Hall's Coaches of Hounslow, Middlesex, ordered a Duple-bodied Regal for delivery in 1935, a second detachable roof luggage carrier was specified to cater for contracts to carry military bands that were an important part of this operator's business. Mr Charles Hall recalls that, in practice, it was never removed, and that this vehicle was used when his family moved house from Somerset to Surbiton in 1948. The vehicle was broken up after 21 years service with the same firm, in 1956. The basic body design was that same as the top vehicle on this page, but with a wide centre-entrance door, a return to conventional slim window pillars and a simplified front-end.

Surrey Motors Ltd of Sutton was a Regal and Harrington customer from the early 'thirties to the end of this combination [and onwards through the Reliance era]. This picture posed on the Hog's Back near Guildford, shows pairs of vehicles delivered, from left to right, in 1935, 1934 and 1933, the newest being of the stepped-waistrail style.

Burlingham had developed from the 1934 styles to produce this more distinctive design for the 1935 season. The paired windows with shorter bays at front, centre and rear allowed for alternative entrance positions in any of these locations. This example for Brownings of Whitburn appears to have had a tartan waistrail.

This 1935 Regal was another addition to the Keith & Boyle fleet, this time for the London-based Orange Luxury business. The Duple body was quite different from any of those shown opposite, but the rear end had much in common with the KD design introduced at about that time on Bedford chassis. Although not perhaps as well proportioned as some other Duple products of the time, its front end was a foretaste of later designs. More significant from a technical viewpoint was the use of the new A171 7.7-litre oil engine, fitting into the same bonnet space as the petrol engine used in the other coaches on these two pages.

By mid-1935, Huddersfield had decided to standardise on the Gardner 6LW oil engine for its future buses, though retaining the AEC chassis with fluid flywheel and preselective gearbox [the latter now being of AEC manufacture, incidentally]. AEC can hardly have been enthusiastic about this policy but evidently considered the business still worthwhile. The installation was based on that of some similarly-powered AEC Renown six-wheel double-deckers built for LGOC in 1932. The radiator was mounted considerably further forward than ever for the 8.8-litre engine, the effect on this vehicle's proportions being if anything even more noticeable on a single-decker. The first vehicle to this specification, on chassis number O6621742, is seen here — it was one of three with Park Royal bodywork generally similar to that on the petrol-engined vehicles supplied the previous year, though the tail end was shortened to keep the overall length within the 27ft. 6in. limit then applicable. Note that this vehicle, having an odd number, was owned by the LMS railway — even-numbered vehicles were owned by the Corporation.

By contrast, the 7.7-litre AEC oil engine newly adopted as the standard diesel power unit for the Regal in 1935 fitted into the standard front-end as used for petrol models — even the bonnet panels were retained unaltered though the extensively louvred side was probably unnecessarily well ventilated. For a brief period the ''Oil engine'' lettering on the radiator was retained, but the absence of starting handle was otherwise the only external clue visible from any distance — the 7.7-litre engine generally had only a short splined shaft projecting through the radiator,

which, incidentally, was capable of punching a neat hole in the rear panel of the bus in front if a driver misjudged how close he was when parking. The Northern vehicle shown was the first of five placed in service in August 1935, the 36-seat Weymann bodywork being largely of that builder's usual style as built from about 1932 apart from such BET specification features as the destination indicator. New Pickering bodywork was fitted in 1946 and the batch remained in service until 1955, all but one going to Jamaica. Note the revised mudguard design.

Another variety of Regal appeared for the November 1935 Show. This was the Regal Mark II, which had a completely new six-cylinder oil (or, alternatively later, petrol) engine of 6.75-litres capacity (though called '6.6-litre') and modernised frontal appearance with a slightly smaller chromium-plated radiator shell and front mudguard extended forward to cover the front dumb iron, though the final shape was slightly different to that on this prototype chassis. The Autovac fuel-lift device also disappeared from the dash panel.

The first Regal Mark II was given the chassis number O862001, thus starting a new series. It had been rebuilt from an O662-type Regal chassis, reputedly O6621781 — the frame of the new model was generally similar. It was fitted with Weymann 34-seat bodywork and displayed in Rhondda livery as shown on the AEC stand at the 1935 Commercial Show, the last to be held at Olympia in London. It was placed in service by the Rhondda Transport Co Ltd in February 1936 — eight similar vehicles following a few months later. Note that the Regal Mark II lettering did not appear on the radiator of this or subsequent examples — the slatted grille was to be adopted on other models but not until some time later. The bonnet side panel had no access holes and a single row of louvres reminiscent of 1930 practice on 662-type Regals. The vehicle was rebodied by Longwell Green Coachworks of Bristol in 1946 and withdrawn in 1952, passing to an independent operator until being scrapped in 1955.

Just how quickly vehicles could appear out-of-date is conveyed by this picture of petrol-engined Regal 6621725 which was placed in service, registered ANY 28 by D. Davies (Ynysybwl Motor Service) earlier in 1935. The 32-seat body, by Metcalfe, was of a style that would have appeared up-to-date in say 1932 but had now become quite old-fashioned. As it happened, this operator's business was taken over by Rhondda in April 1936 and the vehicle became No. 144 in that fleet, thus joining the vehicle shown above. It was withdrawn in 1948 and also passed to an independent operator, running until 1954.

The centre-entrance layout was evidently judged to be the fashionable trend at the 1935 Show so far as coach bodywork was concerned, although in fact only a minority of operators adopted this layout subsequently. Another development was the adoption of 'streamlined' mudguard outlines as adopted on private cars. For a brief period, no self-respecting bodybuilder seemed content to accept the standard units as supplied by AEC, though very often it was evident that these were built into the final concoctions no doubt by a process of cutting and welding.

Harrington's display included the 7.7-litre oil-engined Regal for the Grey-Green fleet show above. This general style of bodywork was for some years the concern's standard, though with front entrance and normally on Leyland Tiger chassis. Something of the grace of the Harrington design of two years earlier had gone, being replaced by a rather heavy-looking style. The elaborate destination box display was for some years characteristic of Grey-Green coaches, a tradition that was to be revived in the more recent past. The 'registration' number was, of course, for display only.

Among the Burlingham exhibits was the petrol-engined Regal shown below. This was an example of an entirely new Burlingham coach design that was to be popular in the next two years or so, although again almost always with front entrance. The Show exhibit, on chassis 6621761, was Cumberland Motor Services Ltd No. 74 [registered BAO 74] and seated 31.

More representative production versions of Harrington and Burlingham coach bodywork built in the 1936 season are shown above and below. Timpson's need for new coaches in the late 'thirties was relatively limited but the example illustrated, above, is representative. The half-canopy front-end was becoming increasingly popular for coaches in general and was normal for this general design. At the rear, Harrington's 'dorsal fin', partly a styling feature and partly quite an advanced ventilation aid, is just visible above the general roof level. The dorsal fin had been introduced at the time of the 1935 Show; a rakish-looking fully-fronted coach for United Service Transport Co was evidently used as a demonstrator. Another example [right] was built in the early months of 1936 for F. Manning & Sons of Aberdare. The front-end incorporated a special access door for engine maintenance that had been taken up by AEC, whose Chief Engineer favoured development of the full-width cab because of the sym-

metrical appearance which it produced. The Regal below for A. Rimes & Sons, still officially the Swindon Motor Charabanc Co, was typical of Burlingham 1936-37 production in its nicely-proportioned appearance. It was registered AAM 192.

[Above] Several independent operators in the Potteries area took delivery of Regal Mark II models. Brown's Motor Co [Tunstall] Ltd placed two in service early in 1936, the chassis number of this one, O862051 indicating that a half-century had been reached in sales by that time, a reasonably encouraging figure, but subsequent sales slowed markedly. Duple built the neat-looking 39-seat bodywork, taking full advantage of the model's shorter bonnet to give maximum seating capacity. The concept of giving what was really a service bus coach-style exterior trim was becoming common practice among independent operators.

There was still plenty of variety among body-builders and a small concern in Ealing, West London, R.E.A.L. Carriage Works Ltd, bodied this Regal, ATJ 46, for Mercer's Tours of Longridge, near Preston, of which the proprietors were George and Elizabeth Hardacre. The R.E.A.L. concern, which took its name from the Managing Director, Richard E. Allmann, developed this full-front style in the mid-'thirties, lending distinction to an otherwise unremarkable design.

The bodybuilder of this Regal for Beauchief Coaches of Sheffield was Cravens Railway & Carriage Works Ltd of that city. The basic inspiration is clearly the Burlingham 1935-season design, traces of the latter's practice being seen in the destination indicator, side moulding and side window treatment, though the three thicker pillars with oval-shaped embellishments were a Cravens feature.

[Above] Duple had not been idle in the flurry of fresh thinking in coach design in 1935; the first example of this style, destined to set the pattern for the next fifteen years, had been on a Leyland Tiger chassis. However, it suited the Regal if anything even better, as shown by this example supplied early the following year to Batten's of East Ham. The combination of curved waistrail and roof lines with sloping pillars and a curved cab profile was later to become accepted practice, but this original concept was, in the author's view, exceptionally elegant — not only would it have looked completely up-to-date until 1950 but stands as one of the most attractive coach designs of any period.

[Right] With hindsight, it seems strange that a Duple customer did not choose the style shown above, but doubtless in 1936 it looked a little too 'advanced' for more conservative tastes. R. M. Lee of Hertford chose this alternative with almost straight waist and stepped cab front — well up to typical standards for early 1936 but lacking any great styling flair.

At almost exactly the same date, the Midland General Omnibus Co Ltd placed in service ten Regals with Weymann 32-seat bodywork of this style, characteristic of this operator and the associated Mansfield District concern, both in those days part of the Balfour, Beatty group. The inset entrance door was in most fleets a 'bus' feature, but these were coaches and, like the other 662-type Regals on this pair of pages, on petrol-engined chassis. Immaculately maintained in MGO's distinctive blue and cream livery, six, including No. 161 [CRA 660] seen here, survived with the company until 1959, though converted to oil in 1949 and reseated for bus duties. The remaining four were impressed by the War Department in 1939-40, not returning to MGO.

The Green Line business had become part of the empire of the London Passenger Transport Board following the latter's formation in 1933, though retaining its distinctive livery and fleetname. A large and varied fleet of coaches had been acquired with the business of independent concerns operating express services in the LPTB area and it was those of non-standard types that were selected for replacement in 1936 by a batch of 50 new Regals, O6621952-2001. These were the first new vehicles for Green Line since 1931, and most of the ex-independent Regals added to the fleet were of similar age, though a few dated from 1932. Hence the arrival of T403-452, which were generally known by their classification 9T9, was quite an event, especially as they were of very different specification. The chassis, with 7.7-litre engines and preselective gearboxes, were directly equivalent to the Board's STL double-deckers then entering service in large numbers. The 30-seat bodywork, built by Weymann, was in the style which was to become characteristic of Green Line coaches of the later 'thirties, designed by a London Transport team led by Eric Ottaway and having obvious affinity to both the Q type central area buses then entering service [see Best of British Buses No. 2] and the famous RT-type double-deckers that were to follow.

The 9T9 coaches tended not to inspire the widespread regard earned by their successors, the 10T10 coaches, despite being so similar apart from the smaller-capacity engine and the curious built-up bonnet design, perhaps the only styling feature which did not look 'right'. They were all withdrawn by 1951-52. Seen here in their latter days, working on bus routes, are (above) T452, the last of the batch, on a Central Area service, and (right) T414, seen in the Woking area.

After relatively buoyant sales in 1934-35, the market for the Regal 4 dwindled sharply in 1936, no doubt partly because the Regal Mark II was an alternative approach to the idea of a less powerful version of the 'standard' Regal. Burnley, Colne & Nelson Joint Committee took delivery of two oil-engined examples with 35-seat bodywork by Park Royal, this being O642166, seen here among the disused tracks of a former tram depot — a typical scene in numerous municipal undertakings.

[Above] There were two Regal Mark II demonstrators, O862002 [registered as CHX 834] and O862035, the latter being seen here before receiving its registration number EMF 94. In the design of the Weymann body it was a replica of the vehicles built for Rhondda, as shown on page 43, but was evidently supplied in a grey livery, as was not uncommon practice for AEC demonstrators at that time. It is shown lettered ready for a spell with the Southern National Omnibus Co Ltd, evidently newly delivered from the bodybuilders in the early summer of 1936. No Regal Mark II vehicles were sold to either SNOC or the closely-associated Western National company. However, there was a close link with the Bristol Tramways & Carriage Co Ltd, technically at that time a subsidiary of WNOC, although all three were members of the Tilling group, and this vehicle may have influenced the choice of the AEC '6.6-litre' six-cylinder engine for some Bristol JO6A coach chassis.

[Centre] About eighteen months later, and EMF 94 is seen back at Southall, still in grey livery [which had saved the cost of attempting to put it into successive operator's colours] but bearing the Ribble fleetname. Apart from looking slightly travel-stained the appearance of a starting handle where hitherto there had been none suggests that it may have been converted to petrol and could thus be considered as having acted as a temporary prototype for the fleet of Regal Mark II coaches placed in service by Ribble's subsidiary, W. C. Standerwick & Co Ltd in 1938-39. These were petrol-engined, as were most of the later Regal II models, and had Burlingham bodywork of characteristic Ribble design of the period. However, this vehicle was sold to Baker of Warsop. Note the London Transport trolleybus in the background.

[Right] Little publicity was given to the existence of the A174 petrol version of the 105 mm by 130 mm engine used in the Regal II. In fact, the first detailed description did not appear until April 1939. It shared the basic design of the oil engine and was thus unusual among AEC petrol engines in having push-rod operation for the overhead valves. Note the downdraught carburettor, another feature not found on other types of Regal petrol engine.

The contrast between traditional and modern ideas in body design was often very marked in the mid-'thirties. Strachans, for example, produced this pair of widely varying styles within a week or two of each other in the early summer of 1936. For Costin's of Dunstable, ANM 24 had bodywork which would not have looked out of place three years earlier, apart from some superficial details. Though 'dignified', such a design was beginning to look outdated even before it was built and yet lacked the graceful lines of some earlier coaches from the same builder.

By contrast, Valliant Direct Coaches of Ealing, London W5, carried flamboyant styling to extremes on DMX 285. The idea of hiding the radiator behind a grille forming part of the bodywork had been used for a year or two on some American cars. In this case the grille was almost a caricature of the standard outline visible directly behind it, on which even the Regal script had been left undisturbed. Understandably, the starting handle had been removed; the chassis was petrol-engined and would therefore have been so fitted as standard. The pronounced windscreen rake did not marry too happily with the lines of the rest of the vehicle and its high sill level must have worsened forward vision for both driver and passengers.

Another out-of-the-ordinary design was this Park Royal body for Birmingham Co-operative Society Ltd, registered COB 77 and dating from June 1936. In general, the design was restrained and unpretentious but the omission of any destination or illuminated name panel gave a curiously old-fashioned look to the front-end; indeed the absence of fleetname was itself unusual. The entrance door position, set back by one bay from the front had been fairly popular a few years earlier but was rare at that date. An interesting detail was the semaphore-type direction indicator mounted over the Autovac — these were coming into common use on cars at that date and for a time were fairly common on coaches, sometimes being built into the bodywork.

Although Rover Bus Services of Aberdeen had sold part of its operation with five vehicles [including two AEC Q single-deck buses] to Aberdeen Corporation in November 1935, the business continued and this Regal with petrol engine was placed in service the following year. The bodywork is believed to have been built by Walker, also of Aberdeen.

[Above] Green's Motors Ltd of Haverfordwest operated fifteen vehicles, mainly Leylands, on a network of services in that part of Pembrokeshire sometimes known as 'little England beyond Wales', where this attractive background was found when photographing the Park Royal-bodied oil-engined Regal delivered in June 1936. Green's continued in operation until taken over by Western Welsh in 1957.

[Below] Duple's interpretation of a full-fronted coach in the 'modern' idiom of the time appeared towards the end of 1936. A particularly harmonious effect was created by adopting the curved cab profile introduced a year earlier, modified so as to bring the front panel almost flush with the radiator at the bottom, though the body design as a whole differed from the previous curved-waistrail style in being of '4½-bay' rather than four-bay layout behind the entrance door. The vehicle was completed for the Scottish Show, painted in a light blue metallic finish [itself a new development at the time] for operation by Leamington Touring Services Ltd of Blackpool. FV 8194 was later sold to Grange Motors of Grange-over-Sands, retaining the same livery.

City of Oxford Motor Services Ltd was a regular customer for Regals from 1931 to 1950 [and until 1952 if the underfloor-engined Mark IV model is included]. In the 'thirties, body orders were placed with either Park Royal or Weymann, and although the designs changed gradually in accordance with prevailing trends, the respective styles adopted were often very similar. The 1937 batch of fifteen Regals had 32-seat bodies built by Weymann — much the same design was produced up to 1940. This picture of EFC 286 on chassis O6622106 was taken in post-war days but, as was typical of Oxford buses in their distinctive livery of red, maroon and duck-egg green, it was still in smart condition. By that date the fleet number was simply 9; in 1937 it had been J9, the J indicating that it had the original direct-injection A171 7.7-litre engine, later altered to JD9 when converted to direct injection, until 1946 when the prefix was dropped. It was withdrawn in 1952 but was then operated by Reliance of Newbury until 1958.

Chapter Five : The late 'thirties and a revival of Regal success

It seems to have been realised by 1937 that the Regal Mark II was not going to be a commercial success (though its engine was later to be the basis of the power unit in the original version of AEC's most successful single-decker of all, the underfloor-engined Reliance introduced in 1953). The standard Regal was given a minor face-lift in terms of appearance that year, by which date it had become clear that it was going to remain the main AEC single-decker for the remainder of the 'thirties; about 400 examples had been sold in 1935-36. The 7.7-litre A171 oil engine attracted new customers, such as the Northern Ireland Road Transport Board, itself newly-formed, which put 40 Regals of this type on the road in 1936.

London Transport made its first new additions to the T class that year with 50 Green Line coaches also having the A171 unit but with the AEC-built preselective gearbox, at that stage relatively uncommon on a Regal except for municipal examples. These were the 9T9 class vehicles which were an indicator of London Transport's reversion to relatively orthodox single-deck design after the brief period of choice of the side-engined AEC Q for its single-deck requirements, and set the standard for late 'thirties Green Line body style with their Chiswick-designed but Weymann-built bodywork.

Until about 1937 the British Electric Traction group constituents had been rather cool on orders for Regals,

with limited exceptions from such concerns as City of Oxford Motor Services Ltd (though even that concern had favoured Leyland Lions in 1934). However, from then, BET companies figured more strongly in the Regal order lists, with batches in 1937 for Trent (20 vehicles), Rhondda (12) and Northern General (35), the last-mentioned being unusual, particularly for this group, in having preselective gearboxes.

Orders for independent operators continued to concentrate on petrol-engined models and a handful of orders for chassis to be bodied as coaches for larger concerns also called for petrol engines. However, the emphasis was on the 7.7-litre engine and a new development, the direct-injection A173 version using a toroidal combustion chamber, particularly appealed to major company fleets. This had been quietly introduced in 1936 but not publicly announced until 1938. It improved fuel consumption and although power output was down — early examples developed 90 bhp at 1,750 rpm — in stopping bus service, the difference was not particularly noticeable.

However, not only the A171 engine but the 8.8-litre in its A165 form as built from 1932 continued to be available, and the latter was still specified by municipalities such as Sheffield, Salford and Halifax either needing power for hilly routes or standardising on the same engine as used in contemporary Regents. Huddersfield, however, took an individual line on engine policy by specifying the Gardner 6LW unit. The AEC works was busy with the production of Regents and also trolleybuses in the late 'thirties, many of them required for tramway replacement schemes, but Regal output also rose. About 1,000 examples were built in 1937-38, a rate of output similar to that in the early days of 1929-31.

Once again this figure was due to a considerable extent to a London order, for London Transport placed a contract for some 266 more Regals — the largest total covered by a single order — for its Green Line fleet, intended to replace the early Regals on these limited-stop services and those vehicles acquired from independent operators which had not already been withdrawn. The chassis were numbered O6622600-2865, being numbered in sequence T453-718. The chassis had yet another engine variant, the A180, a direct-injection version of the 8.8-litre using the pot-cavity combustion system that had been standardised since 1933 by

Leyland, giving particularly smooth running if not quite the efficiency of the toroidal version. A slightly more compact installation of the 8.8 was possible in this form and these vehicles had a particularly neatly-designed frontal appearance, suiting the stylish if rather heavy-looking Chiswick-built body. These vehicles, classified 10T10, were to remain the backbone of the Green Line fleet until replaced by an almost exactly similar number, 263, of the underfloor-engined RF-class Regal IV model.

Even so, the Regal was doing well in other markets, with further orders for BET companies which now again included some from Devon General. There were even a few for fleets which had come under Tilling management, such as a total of 34 for the Bristol Tramways & Carriage Co (in those days the makers of Bristol buses) and its associate Bath fleet and also the Royal Blue business which had become part of the Western and Southern National Omnibus Cos. Another more regular company group customer for Regals at this date was the Balfour Beatty combine, the main fleets concerned being Midland General and Mansfield District.

SMT remained a regular customer and its 1938 and 1939 orders for fifteen and twenty vehicles brought the total of Regals and closely associated types placed in service in this fleet since 1930 and given B-series fleet numbers to 214. Most were still in service, and formed the largest fleet of Regals outside London, despite SMT being the only company in the Scottish group to operate large numbers of AEC buses. It has to be said that even in this fleet, they were outnumbered by the ubiquitous Leyland Tiger.

In England, the Northern General Transport Co Ltd, which had turned from an intermittent to a committed

Regal customer, placed 53 examples of a variant which was at first peculiar to this concern in service between May and July 1939. They had the 7.7-litre direct-injection engine and a new more compact front-end layout, with the driving position moved as far forward as possible, using a more upright steering column. This allowed the front bulkhead also to move forward to allow sufficient body space for surprisingly comfortable seats, at least for medium-height occupants, to be provided for 38 passengers, a total hitherto not possible on a standard Regal. The rear-end of the cylinder block protruded slightly through the bulkhead, being covered by a small cowl. (It has been said that these vehicles were prone to boiling, as the fan had been eliminated, also in the interests of reducing the bonnet length. However, my recollections as a youthful but keenly observant passenger when they were anything up to about nine years old include no memories of any such incidents despite several trips in the hillier parts of West Durham. Maybe some of them succumbed to furring of radiators with the hard local water in their later years when many had the original bodies replaced and remained in service until well into the 'fifties.) A further 32 similar vehicles were supplied in 1940, plus a few more for NGT's Tynemouth subsidiary and chassis of almost identical specification were used for SMT's 1940 delivery of 20 Regals. These latter had Alexander 39-seat body-work as used on the Leyland Tiger TS8 Special vehicles delivered to most SMT group companies in 1939-40. The first few NGT Regals of this type to be registered dated from a month earlier than the first Alexander TS8 Specials, so it seems possible that NGT and AEC could claim the credit for this ingenious

Aberdeen Corporation, after a period when the side-engined AEC Q had been in favour, adopted the Regal as its principal choice for single-deckers in the late 'thirties. The first of the 1937 batch, No. 124 [RG 8124] on chassis O6622285, is seen when new. The specification included 7.7-litre engine, preselective gearbox and a somewhat utilitarian style of 35-seat body built by the local Walker concern and having an unusual 'slim' style of front canopy, complete with a rather flimsy-looking diagonal stay rod. Also in the depot yard visible are the upper-deck of one of the Walker-bodied Crossley double-deckers and, in the background, what appears to be the lower deck of a double-deck tram. Aberdeen considered it unnecessary to indicate to which city its municipal buses belonged, except in the small lettering of the undertaking's address.

idea, which gave front-engined vehicles a seating capacity only one or two short of the maximum possible with an underfloor or side engine within the same 27ft. 6in. length limit. It seemed a pity that such ingenuity tended to be forgotten after the war, though NGT did have some similarly-arranged Guy Arab single-deckers in 1947.

However, to complete the picture of Regal progress in the late 'thirties, orders from municipal and independent operators continued to play their part in the overall picture. Both Liverpool and Glasgow Corporations had been regular customers for Regents for some years and chose the Regal for single-decker contracts in 1939-40, though not all of the Glasgow batch of 30 were delivered due to the outbreak of war. The longer-established business from the Yorkshire undertakings at Halifax, Huddersfield and Sheffield continued, each with its own distinctive specification. Independent operators also continued to order Regals often in ones or twos, for delivery up to 1939 and as had been the case right through the 'thirties, chose a wide variety of body designs — mostly coaches — for them.

Delivery of Regals, even to non-standard design, did not immediately cease after the war began in September 1939 though it seems probable that regular chassis production did not continue for long. Bodied vehicles continued to arrive in operators' fleets until the summer of 1940 and there were one or two instances

of newly-delivered chassis or vehicles being stored until after the war. Westcliff-on-Sea Motor Services Ltd took delivery of three petrol-engined Duple 30-seat coaches (6623400-2) in 1939 but did not register them until 1946 as BJN 116-8, thus placing in service what were almost certainly the last AEC petrol-engined passenger vehicles.

Some orders were cancelled and numerically the last of the 'pre-war' series to be placed in service in Britain appear to have been the 1940 SMT batch (O6623582-3601) although the following two chassis, O6623602-3, apparently turned up after the war with Lancashire independents. At least one later export order was completed and the chassis concerned, O6623632, built for Baghdad, helped to lay the foundations for one of AEC's most consistent series of post-war export contracts.

Cancelled orders account for large gaps in the Regal chassis number series but the numbers O6623897-3903 were allocated to rebuilds of Regal Mark II (862 model) chassis carried out for Sheffield United Tours.

Export business, which had played a relatively small though steady part in Regal sales from the beginning, began to become more important in the late 'thirties. Some of this came from countries within what was then called the Empire and understandably in those days following British practice in their choice of vehicles. Thus, the Transport Board of Sydney, Australia, specified thirteen Regals to go with 37 Regents ordered in 1937,

and others went to New Zealand and South Africa.

However, some noteworthy orders were secured from markets where competition from other countries could be expected to be strong, despite the absence of a left-hand drive model. Admittedly, an order from Athens for 60 Regals fulfilled in 1938 was partly due to the operation of transport in that city by a British company, though the vehicles were of technical interest in having a special small-bore version of what was basically the 8.8-litre engine, but with a bore size of 103 mm and thus having a swept volume of 7.0 litres. The chassis wheelbase was 19ft. instead of the usual 17ft. 6in. and the vehicles had fluid flywheels preselective gearboxes and Metro-Cammell fully-fronted bodies carrying 70 passengers, of which 33 were seated.

South America was already becoming an important market, and in 1937 Regal chassis began to be supplied to Co-operative Bus Services in Montevideo, where buses were then usually based on chassis from the United States. By May 1938, AEC announced that 125 vehicles — mostly if not all Regal — were in service or on order for this organisation. No doubt most, if not all, had arrived by the time of the dramatic days of the Battle of the River Plate fought nearby between the German pocket battleship Admiral Graf Spee and ships of the Royal Navy in the early months of the 1939-45 war.

A face-lift — or perhaps it should be called a 'face-drop' — was applied to AEC passenger models towards the end of 1937 when the deeper radiator and modified front wing and dash panel covering the front dumb irons first appeared. This photograph of a petrol-engined chassis dates from October of that year. Production vehicles carried the process further by the adoption of bonnet panels without louvres for oil-engined chassis and the large chromium-plated front hub caps, both features only retained for a limited period. Clearly the intention was to up-date the appearance and, apart from minor details, the appearance of the 662-series Regal was not significantly to alter until production ceased in 1947. Thus with these quite modest changes, the original concept of 1929 was able to remain up-to-date looking over a production run of some eighteen years during a time of great changes — a remarkable tribute to its basic soundness.

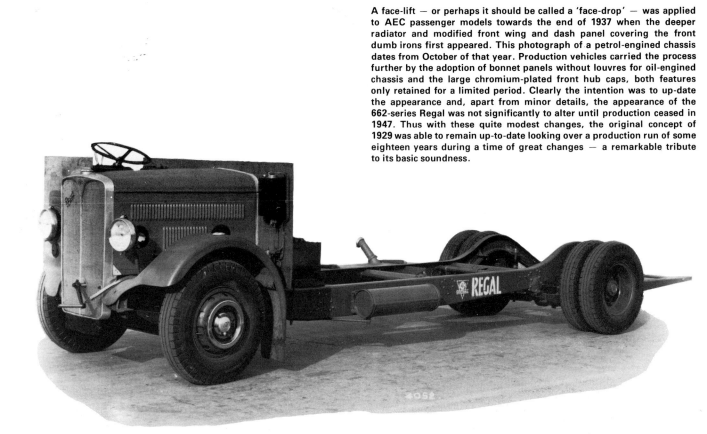

[Above] The Bath Tramways Motor Co Ltd came into the empire of the then Bristol Tramways & Carriage Co Ltd and hence the Tilling group in December 1936. Although a new batch of 20 vehicles delivered in 1937 maintained previous policy in being based on Regal chassis, though now oil-engined, the bodywork showed Tilling influence in being by Eastern Coach Works Ltd — the subsidiary newly formed to take over Eastern Counties coachbuilding activities. The body design, apart from the use of rear entrance layout, had quite a strong resemblance to contemporary vehicles for the West Yorkshire Road Car Co Ltd, including the style of destination indicator. The photograph taken later in 1937 conveys the atmosphere of the city — note the tram track on the left. Cars visible include contemporary Riley and Hillman Minx models and what could be an Alvis in a side street. No. 2226, on chassis O6622317, saw further service in Wales after withdrawal in 1951, being scrapped in 1959.

[Below] Independent operators continued to comprise a significant proportion of Regal customers, almost invariably for petrol-engined chassis with the standard 'crash' gearbox. Here an example supplied to Essex County Coaches Ltd of Leyton in the eastern outskirts of London in the Spring of 1937, is seen loading before departure on a Worker's Travel Association tour soon after entering service. Essex County was the regular operator of WTA tours, a venture designed to encourage travel among people who hitherto had often ventured no farther than the nearest seaside resort. The bodywork on EVW 790 has many Harrington-like characteristics but some of the details and contours raise doubts in the author's mind as to which concern had built it. The poster on the left refers to special Coronation-time excursions by the steamer Golden Eagle.

The Northern General Transport Co Ltd was stepping up its orders for Regals. The entire 1937 intake of new vehicles consisted of 35 examples with 34-seat bodywork to a BET Federation design which bore obvious resemblance to the style built in large quantities on Leyland Tiger chassis for other BET-associated fleets but was not so low-built, the rear rows of seats being at a slightly raised level. The body contract was split between Weymann [20 vehicles] and Brush [15]. The 7.7-litre oil-engined chassis were unusual in a BET fleet at that time in having preselective gearboxes. No. 737 [CN 7952] on chassis O6622212 is seen here at Southall before delivery — an error had been made in applying the NGT company body number 905 instead of the fleet number to the bonnet. This vehicle remained in service until 1954.

In terms of new vehicles, the end of the road for the Regal 4 came in 1937, when Swindon Corporation took delivery of what were to be the last chassis numerically, O642176-178, becoming that undertaking's numbers 1 to 3 and registered AWV 555-7. Most records show these vehicles as having fleet and registration numbers in sequence, but this official Park Royal picture shows No. 1 as AWV 557, that concern having built the 37-seat centre-entrance bodywork. The Regal 4 continued to be listed as available until 1940, though no further orders were fulfilled.

David MacBrayne Ltd, operating road and sea services in the Western Highlands, had been a Regal operator since 1934, but in 1937 there first appeared examples with what was to be the characteristic style of bodywork associated with that operator's examples of the model. Built by Park Royal, it was in keeping with contemporary coach styling with a slightly curved waistrail, even if the interpretation was not as free-flowing as those of the specialist coach bodybuilders of the day. This was one of three completed in March 1937.

Orange Bros Ltd, of Bedlington, which had emerged as the leading independent operator on the Newcastle-London service, was acquired by Tilling & British Automobile Traction Co Ltd in August 1934 and although operated thereafter as a part of United Automobile Services Ltd, it remained a separate company. It was probably in fulfilment of an outstanding order that five Regals were purchased in 1937. These had 30-seat rear-entrance bodywork built by Brush to a design which was virtually identical to the Burlingham 1935 style which had been adopted by United, usually with Leyland Tiger chassis, as its standard long-distance coach. The last of the batch, on chassis O6622382, is seen at Victoria Coach Station in London when comparatively new — originally

it had been delivered as ARO 14 but within a year or so became ARO 34 in a renumbering of the various Regals, mainly second-hand, in the United and Orange fleet. Despite their name, Orange Bros had favoured a rather sombre livery of brown and khaki, and this was retained under the new ownership. The fleet number prefix indicated 'AEC Regal Oil', and these vehicle had 7.7-litre engines, United evidently favouring retention of the starting handle usually found only on petrol examples. The batch, by then in the main United fleet, was rebodied as buses by Willowbrook in 1950 and withdrawn in 1955. Note the AEC advertisement behind the vehicle — the vehicles partly visible are also believed to have been Regals, in the Royal Blue fleet.

Uruguay began a long spell as an important export market for Regals in 1936-37, when initial orders placed by Cooperativa Bus Services of Montevideo amounted to 56 vehicles. One of the first is seen in the foreground of this view, in the livery of Organizacion Nacional De Autobuses. The other vehicles seen are mostly, if not all, on American chassis, among those visible being examples of International, Studebaker, Ford and Reo makes. AEC-built vehicles were sold under the ACLO name in South America.

The Scottish Motor Traction Co Ltd was building up its Regal fleet throughout the 'thirties, its B class accordingly having reached B179 with the first vehicle [on chassis number O6622559] in the 1938 delivery of fifteen buses with Alexander 34-seat bodywork which still had the traditional cutaway style of rear entrance. The complete batch was delivered in March 1938. Alexander's standard body design had developed into a particularly distinctive pattern by this date, the cab treatment blending well with the AEC radiator. The SMT livery at the time was two-tone blue and cream and this, too, suited the design well. None of the batch was withdrawn before 1958 and eight that were rebodied by Burlingham as coaches [including B179] survived until 1963-64.

The revised design of front mudguard and the new large chromium-plated front hub cap first appeared on 1937 Show vehicles together with the lengthened radiator. However, a few chassis were built with these features in conjunction with the original short radiator, this example being a petrol Regal, 6622935, one of two placed in service for touring work by Northern General Transport in April 1938. It was not uncommon at that time for petrol chassis to be specified for coaches in fleets generally standardising on diesel, though NGT's next coaches were oil-engined. The Duple body, in the operator's coach livery of cream and maroon, was a combination of contemporary curvaceous lines with traditional-style hinged door and roof luggage carrier. It was the operator's policy to register batches of vehicles in all the main local authority areas in its territory and so although the NGT headquarters were at Bensham, in Gateshead, No. 875 was registered in South Shields as CU 3955 and the small legal lettering gives Chester-le-Street as the address — the company had a traffic office there.

Arguably the most famous Regals of all and the largest single order were the 266 vehicles that comprised London Transport's 10T10 class of Green Line coaches, purchased to replace the original fleet dating from 1930-31 on those services. Based on chassis O6622600-2865 and numbered T453-718 in sequence, they entered service between January 1938 and March 1939, mainly during the spring and summer of 1938. They bore an obvious outward resemblance to the 50 vehicles of type 9T9 placed in service in 1936. However, London Transport was beginning its swing back to the 'big engine' policy and so these vehicles had 8.8-litre engines of a design derived from the A165 unit that had been the standard AEC engine in 1932-35, but with a direct-injection layout derived from contemporary Leyland practice, with pot-shaped piston cavity. On paper, and in relation to the original '8.8', the power was modest — about 100 bhp at 1,750 rpm — but this was deliberately restricted in the interest of engine life and, in practice, these vehicles gave an impression of effortless performance, partly because the engine was particularly smooth-running over most of its speed range despite the lack of flexible mounting. The installation was more compact than that of the standard 8.8, the radiator projecting only slightly beyond the dumb irons, though it continued to be mounted slightly higher than with the 7.7. The engines on the first few vehicles, up to T458, were officially designated A165Z but from thereon were of type A180A. All had preselective transmission. Bodywork, as well as being of LPTB design, was built in the Board's body shops at Chiswick. The vehicles were ordered in two batches and the first 150 bodies seated 30, being of body type T10, the remainder being of 34-seat layout and classified T10/1. Appearance was largely as on the 9T9, but the curious built-up bonnet of the latter gave way to a simpler design. The photographs show [right] T491 and [below] T684 after being overhauled and repainted in the post-war two-tone green livery in 1946.

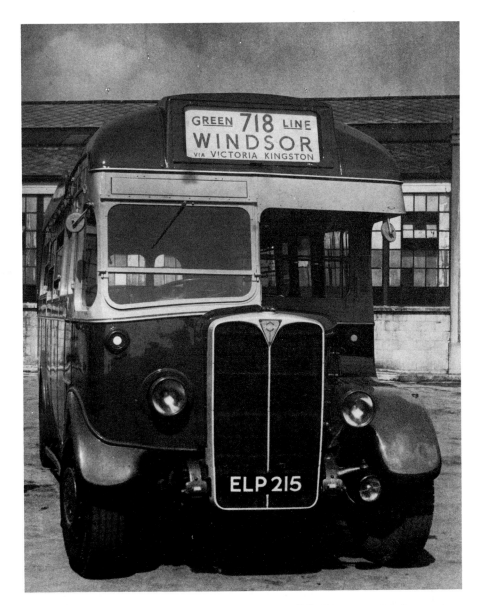

[Above] The appearance of AEC vehicles in the Bath Tramways Motor Co Ltd fleet immediately after its take-over by the Bristol Tramways & Carriage Co Ltd had not been too surprising, but the delivery early in 1938 of a batch of eighteen coaches to the main Bristol fleet must have caused a few eyebrows to be raised as BTCC not only produced almost all its own requirements for bus chassis but by then was the main supplier to companies under Tilling control all over the country. The 32-seat bodywork was built by Duple to an attractive, if restrained, Bristol specification very similar to one used for some coaches on Bristol L5G chassis. The chassis were to 1938 pattern with the longer radiator, etc, the picture also showing the revised design of bonnet side with no louvres standardised for oil-engined models in 1938-39. No. 2095 was on chassis O6622895.

A final batch of three coaches for the Bath fleet was also delivered at about the same time, the first vehicle, No. 2247 being shown. These had bodywork of very similar style, but built by Weymann — an unusual choice of bodybuilder for a Tilling group fleet, but again probably a legacy of the takeover. The chassis, despite being to 1938 specification, had relatively low numbers, O6622039-41, which may have also reflected late completion of an outstanding order, though AEC was in the habit of occasional gap-filling of numbers of vehicles for which orders were cancelled. The body design shows characteristics familiar on contemporary Weymann double-deckers around the cab and rear quarters.

A rather incongruous effect was produced when AEC's new and rather 'glamorous' chassis styling was married with bodywork of more traditional or, not to put too fine a point on it, old-fashioned design. In March 1938, Halifax Corporation took delivery of eleven 7.7-litre Regals with this style of Park Royal 32-seat bodywork, No. 50, on chassis O6622943 being shown.

[Above] Westcliff-on-Sea Motor Services Ltd had been a regular AEC customer in the earlier 'thirties, but the acquisition of the company by Thomas Tilling Ltd in March 1935 was followed by a switch of allegiance to Bristol as chassis supplier for subsequent buses, in the manner usual with that group. However, AEC chassis continued to be favoured for touring or excursion coaches and in addition to some examples of the normal-control Ranger model, Regals were added to the fleet. The vehicle shown, on chassis 6623043, was one of two supplied in 1938, the Duple 30-seat bodywork featuring curved-glass cantrail windows. They were petrol-engined and three similar vehicles delivered shortly after the outbreak of war in September 1939 were stored and not registered until 1946 thus becoming what are believed to have been the last petrol-engined AEC passenger models to enter service.

[Right] By 1938, Burlingham's standard coach design was this four-bay style with gently curving waistline, sloping pillars and, barely visible in this view, a distinctive rear window design, with two large panels set in a vee formation. W. S. Ellison Ltd of St. Helens took delivery of DJ 8294 towards the end of 1938. Note the retention of the louvred bonnet for the petrol-engined chassis.

It had become something of a tradition that Duple would produce something out of the ordinary on a Regal chassis for the Scottish Shows, which took place in even-numbered years in the 'thirties when there was no Earls Court Commercial Motor Show. James Sutherland of Peterhead was again the operator of the examples built for the 1938 Show. This followed a fashion briefly in favour at about that time of providing a panel and front corner pillar on the nearside to give an illusion of a fully-fronted body. As it could be swung out of the way to give access to the bonnet, the usual objections of obstruction to engine maintenance often levelled at the fully-fronted cab were overcome to some degree, though the panel itself with the necessary framing was apt to be cumbersome.

[Above] Export orders continued to roll in, with Empire markets, as they would then have been described, prominent. This Regal for Dunedin City Corporation in New Zealand was placed in service in 1938. The 8.8-litre engine continued to be available and tended to be favoured in export markets where adequate power was thought more important than extreme fuel economy. The bodybuilder is not known, but may have been Dunedin's own workshops, which built bodywork on succeeding Regals. The framework in front of the radiator appears to be a pram-carrier, the pram handle being inserted in the hooks under the top bar — such devices were a characteristic of some New Zealand buses for many years.

[Below] Another user of 8.8-litre Regals was Durban Corporation in Natal, South Africa, though in this case six examples were exported complete with Park Royal bodywork. The proportion of the mudguards suggest 8ft.-wide bodywork — home-market vehicles were confined to 7ft. 6in. at that date and the production of wider chassis was not yet common practice. Note the dark glass in the upper part of the windows. The exhortation "Please have exact fare ready" suggests that the vehicle may have been one-man operated though the exterior of the cab gives no indication of other provision for this.

A minority of home-market customers in addition to London Transport also continued to specify the 8.8-litre engine. Generally these were municipalities, which by nature were perhaps less likely to be influenced by AEC's publicity and its emphasis on the 7.7-litre engine — the 8.8 was hardly mentioned after 1935. However, this Regal supplied to Everingham Bros of Pocklington, East Yorkshire, early in 1938 is noteworthy as having the rare combination of the 8.8-litre unit with the contemporary combination of deeper radiator, new-style mudguards and large front hub caps. Evidently a louvre-less bonnet side had not been produced for this engine at the time. The bodywork was by the local Barnaby concern. Everingham Bros was still operating Regals when the business was taken over by East Yorkshire Motor Services Ltd in 1957.

More typical of an independent operator's choice was 6622989, a petrol-engined model, delivered to E. Howe of Spennymoor, County Durham, in May 1938. However, the choice of body was not so likely for such a fleet, being built by Roe of Leeds to that concern's standard style as supplied to larger companies and municipalities. Howe was the smaller partner in the OK Motor Services organisation running the Bishop Auckland-Newcastle service as well as a network of local routes. The vehicle was impressed for military service during the 1939-45 war and did not return. The Howe business was later taken over by W. Emmerson of Bishop Auckland, the larger OK partner.

[Below] Like almost all major manufacturers, AEC's experimental department had its 'hack' vehicles, used for development work of all kinds and sometimes simply as a convenient form of transport. This photograph, taken in April 1939, shows what was described as an 'experimental car' based on a Regal chassis. The short saloon body had been specially built for AEC in the early 'thirties by Strachans. Most of what can be seen of the chassis appears to be to fairly standard 7.7-litre-engined specification of the mid to late 'thirties though the mudguards are of the rubber type which Dunlop was attempting to popularise at the time. However, the front hub cap is a curious survival, evidently being of the style used for the 1930 season, a typical experimental vehicle idiosyncrasy.

Some backtracking from the 1938 styling features is evident in this picture dated 11th July 1939 showing a Regal chassis. The 'soup plate' hub cap has gone again to be replaced by the familiar AEC style of chromium-plated wheel-nut guard ring and smaller polished hub cap as used since 1931. The bonnet side has also reverted to virtually the mid-'thirties pattern, complete with two rows of louvres, a somewhat surprising alteration as the louvred bonnet was decidely old-fashioned, at least in the more fashion-conscious private car world, by that date and AEC's A173 direct-injection 7.7-litre engine by then standard, was even less likely to need maximum cooling than the A171. Moreover, a louvred bonnet was more prone to cracking and often gave way in such vehicles' later years to simpler operator-manufactured styles. The identity of the vehicle is unknown but the preselective gearbox visible amidships and the straight rear frame suggests a municipal operator, and it was thus probably oil-engined, despite the starting handle. By this date coach chassis invariably had dropped rear extensions giving an appearance like a double-decker chassis.

One of the most ingenious developments of the standard Regal [model O662] chassis was the special 'short-structure' version produced early in 1939 for Northern General Transport Co Ltd. By adopting a more upright steering column and thus moving the driving position forward, it was possible to reposition the front bulkhead of the body to allow provision of seats for 38 or 39 passengers, a capacity hitherto beyond the capabilities of any home-market Regal except the small-engined Regal Mark II. The larger A173 engine of the standard Regal was accommodated by allowing the rear end of the cylinder block to project slightly through the bulkhead. Almost simultaneously a corresponding Leyland Tiger variant was being produced for the SMT group and in 1940 the SMT company itself took delivery of some Regals of the short-structure type. The body design on the 85 Northern General vehicles [and seven more purchased by the associated Tynemouth and District fleet] placed in service between May 1939 and June 1940 was peculiar to this operator, though distinct similarities, particularly in cab design, to bodywork on otherwise quite different vehicles placed in service by Potteries Motor Traction suggest some involvement by either the BET Federation office in London or one of the bodybuilders. The example shown above left, No. 918, was one of the first batch, which had half-drop opening windows, this example being bodied by Brush. Tynemouth No. 118, also with Brush body, was one of those with top-sliding windows, delivered in 1940.

UNIT CHART 1939 PASSENGER MODELS

NAME	MODEL N°	WHEEL BASE	OIL OR PETROL	N° OF CYLS	BORE x STROKE	TRANSMISSION	LIST	ENGINE	PEDAL GEAR	GEAR BOX	EPICYCLIC GEAR BOX	CHANGE SPEED	MID AXLE	REAR AXLE	BRAKE GEAR	CLUTCH	FLUID FLYWHEEL	CARDAN FRONT	CARDAN REAR	TYRE AXLE	FRONT AXLE	STEERING	RADIATOR
REGAL	O662/19	17'-6"	OIL	6	105 x 146 (7.7 LITRES)	STANDARD	BASIC STANDARD	A173	C147	D124	—	E122	—	F184	G218	J138	—	K148	K245	—	L139	M134	N164
						FLUID (S. MOUNTED)	SV54	SV54	SV54	—	D132	SV54	—	F184	SV54	—	J150	SV54	SV54	—	L139	M134	N164
						FLUID (R. MOUNTED)	SV108	SV108	6V108	—	D132	SV108	—	F184	SV108	—	J150 SV108	SV108	SV108	—	L139	M134	SV108
REGAL 'A'	O662/19	17'-6"	OIL	6	115 x 142 (8.8 LITRES)	STANDARD	SV58	A180	SV58	D124	—	SV58	—	F184	SV58	6V58	—	K148	K245	—	L139	M134	SV58
						FLUID	SV61	A180 SV61	SV61	—	D132	SV61	—	F184	SV61	—	J150	6V61	SV61	—	L139	M134	SV61
REGAL 'B'	O662/19	17'-6"	OIL	6	105 x 146	STANDARD	6V97	A173	SV97	D124	—	SV97	—	F184	SV97	J138	—	K148	K245	—	L139	SV97	6V97
REGAL	662/19	17'-6"	PETROL	6	110 x 130 (7.4 LITRES)	STANDARD	SV55	A162 6V55	C147	D124	—	E122	—	F184	SV55	SV55	—	K148	SV55	—	L139	M134	N163 SV55
						FLUID	6V78	A162 6V77	SV78	—	D132B	SV78	—	F184	SV78	J150	—	SV78	SV78	—	L139	M134	N163 SV58
REGAL 4	O642/	17'-6"	OIL	4	120 x 146 (6.6 LITRES)	STANDARD																	
						FLUID																	
REGAL 4	642/	17'-6"	PETROL	4	112 x 130 (5.1 LITRES)	STANDARD																	
						FLUID																	
REGAL MARK II	O862	17'-6"	OIL	6	105 x 130 (6.6 LITRES)	STANDARD	BASIC STANDARD	A172	C160	D124	—	E122	—	F184	G212	J138	—	K506	K259	—	L153	M147	N172
						FLUID																	
REGAL MARK II	862	17'-6"	PETROL	6	105 x 130 (6.6 LITRES)	STANDARD	SV47	A174 SV47	C160	D124	—	E122	—	F184	SV47	SV47	—	K506	K259	—	L153	M147	SV47
						FLUID																	

This reproduction of part of the wall chart used in AEC's drawing office as a key to the parts lists for the range of models as they existed in 1939 graphically illustrates the difference between the Regal range which the Southall works was set up to produce and the public presentation of models available, as published in 'AEC Gazette' and sales brochures, etc. In the latter, the standard Regal was quoted simply as model O662, with 7.7-litre engine; the Regal 4 [O642] and Regal Mark II [O862] with, respectively, four- and six-cylinder 6.6-litre engines were the only other Regal models listed, though it was made clear that petrol-engined versions of all models were also offered and that 'various additions and alternatives to Standard Equipment are available '.

A closer approximation to real life was conveyed by this wall chart, from which it is clear that, for example, no list of units had been compiled for a contemporary Regal 4 [sensibly enough, since none had been ordered for a couple of years], though this could no doubt have been done quickly enough had a demand arisen. On the other hand, the 'standard' Regal, [quoted as model O662/19 (or 662/19 if petrol-engined) to distinguish the 1939 types from previous generations] was quoted and fully-

listed for some eight sub-variants. The basic standard model now had the A173 direct-injection 7.7-litre oil engine and the D124 crash gearbox, but there were also fluid transmission [ie preselective gearbox] variants with both 'solid' and, at least on paper, rubber-mounted engines [the last-mentioned was in effect a single-deck equivalent of the final pre-war batch of London Transport STL-type Regents of the 15STL16 type, though it is doubtful whether any such Regals were actually built]. The designation 'Regal A' covered 8.8-litre chassis, now with the A180 direct-injection version of this engine — the general availability of such a model was never publicised despite its affinity to the 10T10. 'Regal B' was probably the Northern General short-structure variant illustrated opposite. The Regal Mark II models fully listed are self-explanatory, but provision on the chart for fluid transmission variants is noteworthy, even though not fully detailed — no such variant was ever publicised. The SV numbers refer to Standard Variation lists, listing in detail the differences from the appropriate standard model or unit. The arrow indicates an error — J150 should have been in the fluid flywheel column.

Representative of the pre-war series of Regals in its rare final form, this vehicle for Mansfield District Traction Co was actually delivered in 1940 despite the lack of wartime details on this official picture taken at the body-builders. The vertically-slatted radiator was introduced towards the end of 1939, though it was to become more familiar on the immediate post-war models. The chassis, O66233961, was evidently a generally standard O661/19 with 7.7-litre engine, apart from the absence of headlamps — several operators in the more fog-prone Midlands and North favoured a double fog-lamp system for continuous use in those days. The Weymann body was an updated version of the characteristic Midland General/Mansfield District style, with gently curved cab profile — a handsome bus in the idiom of the period.

[Above] Production of Regal chassis virtually stopped within a few months of the outbreak of war in September 1939, although it was not until the latter part of 1940 that the flow of completed examples to operators dried up. Thus Glasgow Corporation took delivery of its only Regals in that year. Only 21 out of the 30 ordered were delivered and the chassis numbers, in a series of smaller batches, suggest that some diversion of orders from other operators had occurred. Weymann built the 35-seat bodywork to a design which had little in common with that built for Mansfield District as shown on the previous page despite both having several characteristic features of this bodybuilder. No. 705, on chassis O6623467, seen when new with wartime headlamp mask, shows an intriguing reversion to the 1938-style front hub-cap, possibly at the operator's request as the same registration number batch also included Glasgow's No. 723, the only Regent RT-type chassis supplied to an operator other than London Transport until after the war, which was similarly equipped. The radiator, with wire-mesh grille, was also of the 1938-39 rather than 1939-40 style. This vehicle was withdrawn by Glasgow in 1956 and saw a further two years' service with independent operators before being scrapped in 1958.

[Below] Although there were no new Regals built during the true 1942-45 'utility' era, wartime controls were still in force when it was announced in 1945 that production of this model was to be resumed. As usual during the wartime era, chassis were allocated to nominated bodybuilders, and so Harrington, generally associated with luxurious coaches, built a batch of buses on the new O662/20 chassis to Ministry of Supply utility specification relaxed only to the extent permitted in 1945, with curved front and rear domes. This specification was clearly based on BET Federation practice, with inset hinged entrance door. Newcastle Corporation, like Glasgow, a Regent operator but not previously owning Regals, took ten, on chassis numbers O6624192-4201, in February-March 1946, one being seen here before lettering. The large destination display panel sat rather uneasily on the austere-looking body style and the author, a native of Newcastle, well remembers his feelings of disappointment at these vehicles' appearance at a time when true post-war styles had already begun to appear.

Down-to-earth transport for under-earth workers. When bus production resumed after the war, the shortage of new vehicles was acute. Trimdon Motor Services Ltd was one of several of the County Durham independent operators to put new Regals of the immediate post-war type, now officially called Regal I, on to colliery services. FUP 783 was one of two examples which entered service early in 1946. The body, again of rather austere design, was built by Thurgood of Ware, Hertfordshire.

Chapter Six : The 0662/20 – no frills but plenty of sales

No Regal chassis were produced during the major part of the 1939-45 war period, when Southall was busy with military production. The small numbers of vehicles delivered in 1940 were to be the last until peacetime — although it proved possible to complete 92 'unfrozen' Regents from parts in stock in 1941-42, there were no corresponding Regals. However, as the war drew to a close, plans for the restarting of AEC passenger vehicle manufacture were made —

the first announcement in March 1945 again made no mention of single-deckers but when production began the first post-war Regents were soon followed by Regals of directly corresponding design.

The new models were respectively of types O661/20 and O662/20. The suffix number system had been in use since 1930 but tended to be treated purely as a convenient way of producing detailed specifications within the works — the service

department rather pointedly ignored it for record purposes, preferring simply to quote major unit numbers, and certainly the frequent variations and non-standard features made it very difficult to follow. However, the urgency of uninterrupted production and the difficulty in obtaining bought-out non-standard parts caused a much tighter policy of standardisation to be adopted in 1945-47, just had been the case in wartime. Operators' need for vehicles gave them no choice

Export chassis were, despite Britain's own needs, a priority in an attempt to earn enough to begin to overcome the immense financial problems caused by the war. This scene shows AEC chassis after unloading at the docks in Montevideo, Uruguay, early in 1946 — most of the chassis are Regal O662/20 models, although there are also some goods chassis.

but to accept standard specifications.

Thus the O662/20 version Regal was invariably built with A173 direct-injection '7.7'-litre engine and crash gearbox. These features, and such details as the style of radiator and bonnet, were virtually identical to those introduced for model O662/19 in 1939, the only difference of any consequence being the introduction of a new-style triple-servo brake system with purely vacuum-mechanical operation rather than the vacuum-hydraulic system standard throughout the late 'thirties. Overall, the specification was in tune with the needs of the time — simple and efficient but not particularly outstanding in terms of refinement.

The corresponding Regent O661/20 had been christened Regent Mark II, a rather inept designation as it differed far less from a standard 1939 Regent, now classified as 'Mark I' by implication, than the variations between the various early and late versions. Even worse, the Regal O662/20 was at first called the Regal Mark II until it was pointed out that there had already been a quite different model, the O862, with this title. Publicity material was hastily amended to read Regal Mark I.

Although the war had been over for about seven months by the time the first Regal O662/20 models were delivered to operators early in 1946, some of the wartime controls were still effective. Allocation of chassis was handled by the Ministry of War Transport and, to some degree, choice and specification of bodywork was still under Ministry of Supply control. Thus most of the first few deliveries had Harrington 34-seat bus bodies complying with the wartime 'utility' specification in its slightly relaxed form as modified towards the end of 1944. This was particularly ironical as Harrington had not built any true wartime utility bus bodies and its peacetime products, even if buses, had tended to be well above average in style and finish.

However, this situation did not last long and by the spring of 1946, Regals with bodywork to good peacetime specification were beginning to come through in quantity. The demand for vehicles after nearly six years of war was immense. No new coaches had been built after the handful delivered in 1940 and the limited numbers of utility buses built from 1942 had included no full-sized single-deckers. So in addition to many faithful users of Regals since the model's early days, unfamiliar names not hitherto associated with AEC appeared in the order lists, though some of these were soon themselves to become regular customers.

The cancellation of orders due to the war caused further gaps in the chassis numbers actually allocated to completed vehicles and the first for a post-war home market vehicle was O6624168, one of a number of early chassis with stylish Duple coach bodywork, although these were not delivered until the spring of 1946, a couple of months or so after post-war Regals with the Harrington bus bodies mentioned above began to appear. From then on, examples with a wide variety of bodywork entered service in sizeable numbers all over the country.

London Transport placed 50 more Regals in service between March and October 1946 and, as usual, the numbers ran in sequence, T719-768 being O6624308-56 in order. However, the design represented a considerable break with LT policy — the chassis were quite standard, with crash gearboxes (a feature not seen on London AEC bus deliveries since the early 'thirties) and even such details as front mudguards and bonnet were of standard O662/20 pattern, quite unlike the distinctive types used on late pre-war London AEC buses. The bodywork, by Weymann, was of a new design, again of manufacturer's rather than operator's standard apart from such details as LT moquette. Its controversial external styling, with a revival of early 'thirties practice in frontal profile, was again a break with London practice. This body design looked more at home in provincial operators' liveries, notably that of East Midland Motor Services Ltd, another early user for whom it may have been developed as a follow-on to that operator's conservative style of the late 'thirties.

Notable among the 'new' Regal operators was W. Alexander & Sons Ltd, which placed 30 in service beginning in July 1946 and then took succeeding batches until there were 82 by the beginning of 1948. Western SMT and its subsidiaries were other Scottish company users and SMT itself took a batch of 50 with a distinctive design of Duple bodywork in 1946-47 and then 25 with Alexander bodies — thus there was a total of well over 200 of Regal O662/20 in this group alone. MacBrayne, in those days not part of the SMT group, also added to its pre-war Regal fleet.

In England, established Regal operators in the BET group, such as Devon General, East Midland, Northern General, Rhondda and Trent were joined by Maidstone & District which though an established AEC user, had favoured the Leyland Tiger in the 'thirties, and Hebble, hitherto a user of Albions for its single-deck fleet. There were relatively few municipal customers but Sheffield received 20 in 1948 and Chesterfield placed four in service at the end of 1946 which were of interest in having Crossley bodywork, hitherto rarely found on other than Crossley chassis, apart from the special case of Manchester Corporation.

Sizeable independent orders helped to swell the total, as did some from overseas, among the earliest being one for the Danish State Railways for 60, smaller numbers going to Australia, New Zealand and South Africa. As early as the spring of 1946, orders for O662/20 were approaching a total of 1,000. The order book was closed when this total reached about 1,500, with nearly 700 of the corresponding Regent, and although deliveries of completed vehicles were still coming through in fair numbers in 1948, chassis production probably ended in 1947. Hence the rate of production, while it lasted, must have been comparable to that of the original 1929-31 period.

Thus the original 662 and O662 chassis number series came to an end, the final chassis being O6625666 though the total number of vehicles built was rather less at 5,286 due to wartime cancellations. This was an impressive total, even though outnumbered by the Regent 661 and O661 figure of 7,892, quite apart from that for comparable Leyland Tiger production which was considerably higher. But the Regal certainly came second in sales of 'full-sized' British single-deckers of the period, an honourable position, and the story was not over yet.

By no means all the early O662/20 chassis received utilitarian bodywork. This example, HLW 985, for the Grey-Green fleet of George Ewer & Sons Ltd was on chassis O6624252 but HLW 981 of the same fleet and with the same style of Duple bodywork was on O6624169, believed to have been numerically the second post-war chassis, the completed vehicle entering service in May 1946. The marriage of the standard post-war Duple A-type body [also known by the design code FS1] to this series of chassis showed that a Regal could still look up-to-date despite the modest changes in chassis appearance since the original 1929 version. These early post-war Duple coaches had seats based on tubular steel frames which didn't quite convey enough luxury image though comfortably shaped. Unfortunately the O662/20 chassis all seemed to suffer from an irritating transmission 'grumble' at about 30 mph — overall, the standard refinement of running was not outstanding and did not really live up to the image created by the appearance.

Horse boxes on passenger chassis were not uncommon in the early post-war era and Vincent of Reading was one of the best-known bodybuilders, as well as entering the coach market. This three-horse box took part in the Motor Jubilee Parade in the summer of 1946.

London Transport's central area single-deck bus fleet was in even more urgent need of new vehicles than its double-deck counterpart at the end of the 1939-45 war. Accordingly 50 Regals with Weymann bodywork were ordered and delivered between April and November 1946. Apart from one or two very minor details such as the type of headlamps, the chassis were standard O662/20, complete with crash gearboxes. Preselective gearboxes would have been greatly preferable to the operator but even London Transport had to accept the standard vehicle in the interests of rapid delivery — fortunately the drivers were used to similar units in the existing vehicles at their garages, dating as they did from 1929-31. The bodywork was also of provincial rather than London style and, indeed, was curiously out of line with most Weymann products since about 1935 in frontal appearance, reverting to a heavily overhung canopy and stepped cab front, reminiscent of the early 'thirties. Seating was originally provided for 35 passengers but this was soon reduced to 33 and latterly again to 32 to give more circulating room inside. Fleet numbers followed directly on the 10T10 series, being T719-768 with chassis O6624307-56, in order. The classification was 14T12. T733 is seen at Muswell Hill.

[Above] Weymann standardised on the same body style for early post-war single-deck orders. This was in line with policy at Metro-Cammell, the other partner in the MCW sales organisation, where the first body designs in each category to go through after the war ended tended to be adopted as the standard for subsequent orders — hence London style trolleybuses in Newcastle and Glasgow and Birmingham-style Daimler double-deck buses in Edinburgh and Newcastle. The front-end design of the Weymann single-decker was more than a little reminiscent of East Midlands Motor Services late pre-war practice, this concern being virtually unique among major companies in not adopting one form or another of flush-fitting windscreen. This 1947 rear-entrance example on chassis O6624937 was for Hebble Motor Services Ltd, previously a user of Albion single-deckers, which was among the BET companies which standardised on AEC in the early post-war period.

[Below] Maidstone & District Motor Services Ltd swung over to AEC as its supplier of single-deck chassis in 1946-48. Some 93 examples of the O662/20 model were added to the fleet, the first 32 being buses with 36-seat bodywork by Beadle to a style very similar to that built by Harrington on an isolated batch of eight Regals placed in service in 1937. SO 9, seen here, was new in November 1946 and based on chassis O6624609.

W. Alexander & Sons Ltd had bodied most of SMT's pre-war fleet of Regals but in 1946 began to build up a sizeable fleet of this model for its own use. Here A28 [AMS 503], on chassis O6624283, is posed in what was the favourite location for the official bodybuilder's pictures during the period when the Alexander coachworks were in Stirling, in front of the famous castle. Alexander's immediate post-war design of body was reminiscent of the 1939-40 style, but had a more pronounced curve to the cab front profile which gave an up-to-date appearance despite the fairly marked peak effect over the windscreen. This was one of 30 Regal I vehicles placed in service by Alexander in 1946, although 20 of these had Burlingham bodywork — by 1948, Alexander had 82 Regal I buses, all of the O662/20 series. Appropriately the type letter A, originally allocated to early small Albion buses, was available for this new AEC fleet.

Another Alexander-bodied Regal I was this example in the fleet of the Londonderry & Lough Swilly Railway Co. Bodybuilding capacity was even more in demand than that for chassis and quite a number of operators turned to second-hand bodywork. The SMT group had carried out a major campaign of converting single-deckers to double-deckers [mainly Leyland Tigers which had originally had Alexander bodywork] and substantial numbers of the single-deck bodies thus rendered surplus found their way on to other chassis, not infrequently new, as in this case. This one is believed to have dated from about 1935, though its appearance was altered somewhat by a new single-panel windscreen and other details.

South America was a particularly important market for AEC [known locally as ACLO] in the early post-war years. Here two directors of the C.U.T.C.S.A. organisation in Montevideo, Uruguay, discuss future plans with a fine model of a Regal — note that at that date right-hand steering was still standard — passenger doors were provided on both sides, Uruguay having recently switched to driving on the right.

Argentina was another part of the South American market in which ACLO buses sold well in the late 'forties. This fully-fronted body built by Empresa Cordoba Oeste shows clear influence of North American styling trends, yet the right-hand steering position, and the characteristic column angle, indicate that underneath lay a Regal I chassis. The radiator grille built into the front of the body was not that on the chassis but reproduced the familiar contours quite faithfully, something which British bodybuilders seemed curiously unwilling to do when fully-fronted styles became fashionable in the UK a year or two later.

[Below] Burlingham's standard early post-war coach largely followed that builder's immediate pre-war design except for the use of an extra window bay. Somehow it did not seem to sit quite so happily on the Regal I chassis as on the Leyland PS1, whereas the opposite seemed the case with the Duple A type, at any rate to the author. This example was for BTS Motorways of Coventry.

[Above] Among the most attractive bus body styles built on the post-war Regal I chassis was Duple's D type. This 35-seat example on chassis O6624584 was one of seven supplied to Newbury & District Motor Services Ltd early in 1947. This operator had come into the Red & White group and, like some other subsidiaries of that group, was standardising on AEC chassis in the immediate post-war period. When Red & White sold out in 1950, Newbury & District came under the wing of the Thames Valley Traction Co Ltd and ultimately disappeared, nowadays forming part of the Alder Valley concern. The photograph was taken in Newbury soon after the vehicle entered service, all the cars in the background dating from the 'thirties.

[Below] Harrington resumed normal coach production in the summer of 1946. This example for Robin Hood Coaches of Nottingham was on an early post-war chassis, number O6624186 and it seems possible that it had originally been allocated on the basis that it would have one of the 'near-utility' bus bodies which formed this bodybuilder's immediate post-war products. Such a vehicle would have been of little use to a coach operator and Harrington switched to its more traditional type of product as soon as possible.

[Above] Hebble's second batch of Regals, delivered in 1947, reverted to this operator's pre-war practice in having bodywork to BET Federation design, in this case built by Roe. Fleet numbers had meanwhile begun a new series beginning at 1, and so O6625453 was No. 14. The livery at this date was crimson, maroon and cream, and these vehicles had quite a smart appearance.

[Left] Brush Coachworks Ltd was still prepared to build bodywork to operator specification. This Regal for Western SMT Co Ltd had bodywork of a rather distinctive style which had first appeared in 1946 on some 1934 Leyland Lion chassis which had been rebuilt as coaches and used on the Glasgow-London service. However, despite its coach livery and 'on tour' destination display, BAG 155 on chassis O6624579, had bus seats for 35 passengers.

Northern General Transport Co Ltd took what could perhaps be regarded as the Brush standard bus design of the period for a batch of eighteen 36-seat buses delivered in 1947. This was the last one, No. 1152, on chassis O6625039, photographed in South Shields soon after entering service in October of that year — for some reason, it had the individual registration number ACN 152, the rest of the batch being CN 9975-91. It was also to prove the swan song of the Regal in the NGT fleet, one of its strongholds from the mid-'thirties, the company favouring Guy chassis for most of its new vehicle needs until 1954 when a return to AEC was made in the Monocoach/Reliance era.

One of the most significant decisions taken in the planning of the Regal Mark III range was the inclusion from the beginning of a left-hand drive version, model 0963, with the engine and other items in mirror-image form as compared to right-hand chassis. AEC had not previously offered a left-hand Regal and it was considered that use of an engine with auxiliaries on the same side as the driving position would make maintenance unsatisfactory. This early Regal III in service with Compania Omnibus Tala S.A. was photographed around 1947/48 in Montevideo; note the Regal I on the left of the picture, with conductor changing the route number. Local body styles in Uruguay retained some characteristics reminiscent of the 'twenties. Justification for the special left-handed chassis was given by sales figures — a total of 1,765 left-hand Mark III passenger chassis was produced between 1946 and December 1957 when production ended [almost all Regal, but including relatively small numbers of Regent III double-deckers] compared to 1,595 of the right-hand Regal III O962 and 9621 series, over the same period.

Chapter Seven : The Regal Mark III

Efforts to produce a 'super' version of the Regent double-decker had begun in 1937, culminating in the RT which appeared on the streets of London in the spring of 1939. The war halted progress beyond the manufacture of an initial production batch of 150 vehicles in 1939-40. AEC publicity kept up the interest in post-war prospects of what became called the Regent Mark III but it was not until 1946 that references began to be made publicly to a Regal Mark III.

Despite the urgent need for new vehicles in Britain, much emphasis was put on exports as a means of putting the country's finances in better shape after the enormous drain on resources of the war. Encouraged by Government policy, manufacturers with export experience were pressed to build up their overseas sales. AEC already had some promising markets and in the early summer of 1946 details were released of the new range, with the emphasis clearly on exports. A new and important feature was a left-hand model, not merely a standard chassis with left-hand steering but a true handed chassis with both the engine and the overall chassis layout to suit countries where traffic drives on the right. This was designated O963, while the right-hand drive models were O962.

Both followed the advanced mechanical design of the RT-based Regent Mark III, with 9.6-litre direct-injection engine (originally derived from a modified version of the 8.8-litre unit) developing 125 bhp and fluid flywheel transmission. The preselective gearbox was controlled through an air pressure system and the brakes were also air-pressure operated. The engine was flexibly mounted — hitherto all production versions of the O662 and 662 Regal had used simple design virtually as introduced in 1929 with the engine insulated from the remainder of the chassis only by a thin strip of resilient material. Alternative wheelbase lengths of 17ft. 6in. or 20ft. were offered for both O962 and O963 models, the longer version being purely for overseas use; UK overall length was still restricted to 27ft. 6in.

Production of Regal Mark III chassis was a little behind that of the corresponding Regent and there was no equivalent of the RT-style Regent chassis for provincial operators built in limited numbers in 1946-47. Few had been built before alternative versions were announced with conventional 'crash' gearboxes (still of the by-then venerable D124 type new in 1931) and vacuum brakes. One of these retained the 9.6-litre engine and was a variant of type O962 while the other incorporated the 7.7-litre unit and this was given a new type number, O682. The latter chassis, though based on the Mark III frame and incorporating its slightly more modern-looking chromium-plated radiator and front-end design, was thus very similar mechanically to the O662/20, the most obvious difference being the flexible engine mounting, which quietened the noise level for passengers appreciably as well as reducing vibration.

Many of the earliest home-market Regal III models, all of which had 9.6-litre engines and fluid transmission, were coaches, this example for Ribblesdale Coachways of Blackburn being on chassis number O962118, placed in service in the latter part of 1947. The 33-seat bodywork was by Trans-United of Rochdale, one of many concerns which entered the coach bodybuilding business during the period of extreme demand shortly after the 1939-45 war. It was one of the most successful and produced some distinctive designs (although this early version had echoes of Burlingham practice, especially at the rear), but like virtually all in this category, faded away in the 'fifties. The front mudguards, with prominent vertical face across the lower edge, were perhaps the most distinctive external feature of the Regal III though the chromium-plated radiator (a feature reminiscent of the Regal II, though that was appreciably smaller) also served to distinguish it from the Regal I. More fundamental, though less obvious, was the characteristic Mark III steering column angle, more nearly upright than on earlier Regals. Early Mark III chassis had the domed front hub caps as used since 1931.

Only quite limited numbers of all three types had been built when in 1948 it was decided to introduce new type designations omitting the 'O' prefix (no longer needed as only oil-engined chassis were offered) but adding a fourth 'series' number (replacing the old 'stroke' number) and a letter to denote transmission type. Thus the standard O962 became 9621E, E denoting 'Epicyclic gearbox'; the O962 with crash gearbox (hitherto officially 'O962 to SV179', the latter being a standard variation number) became 9621A, the A signifying 'AEC' gearbox, and the O682 similarly becoming 6821A. The use of A in this way seems rather amusing in hindsight — it almost suggests that the epicyclic unit was still considered as something of an 'outside' production, despite the fact that AEC had been making its own units of this type since 1934.

As AEC's policy was to issue chassis numbers on receipt of orders for vehicles, long before the order in which they were to be built was decided, this changeover produced some odd effects. Some chassis with early numbers which had not been built had the new-style type prefix, while others with much higher numbers had already been built with old-type designations. Thus what

were nominally the first Regal III models with right-hand steering were 9621E001-005, supplied to East London municipality in South Africa.

Before they had been built, well over 100 chassis with O962 chassis numbers had been produced for the home market alone, with numbers ranging between O962080 and into the 400-plus level. The highest numbered in the author's records are O962414-5, placed in service in May 1948 by Enterprise & Silver Dawn Motors Ltd of Scunthorpe, a sizeable independent operator subsequently taken over by the Lincolnshire Road Car Co Ltd. Like most O962 models, these had epicyclic transmission and the next numbered vehicle, also for E & SD was of similar specification but had the number 9621E416. The lowest-numbered home-market examples were for the Halifax fleet but these were not placed in service until 1949 and were thus 9621E055-67.

London Transport was a comparatively early customer, placing 30 vehicles in service in 1948 and giving them what were to be the last numbers in the T class that had been begun in 1929, T769-798. The first ten chassis in the batch, O962154-163, had O962 prefix letters, but 9621E164-183 were late enough to be caught by

the change in system. These vehicles were, apart from minor details, of standard 'provincial' design, with none of the obvious London Transport features that were already becoming established on the rapidly growing fleet of RT double-deckers. The bodywork intended for country bus service was built by Mann Egerton to a style also used on 100 Leyland Tiger PS1 single-deckers for the central area.

Independent operators were prominent amongst early users of the Regal III. The big company groups, and in particular BET, tended to be more cautious, although such fleets as Rhondda and Sheffield United were represented. It had been BET's persuasion which led to the development of the crash-gearbox versions of the Regent III and Regal III, so it was hardly surprising that interest quickened when these became available, with Devon General and City of Oxford Motor Services Ltd among early users of the 9621A, with some examples of the combined 9621A326-343 series entering service in the summer of 1948.

BET companies also figured strongly in early O682 contracts, and accounted for all the first 83 chassis numbers, with Trent as operators of the first batch (O682001-12, placed in service with Windover coach

All the early publicity relating to AEC's Mark III models was concentrated on the 9.6-litre engine and at first this was the only unit offered. This picture actually shows an A206 engine as fitted to right-hand goods vehicles and thus having a smaller dynamo than the A208 used in early 9.6-litre Regals but it does indicate how the oil bath air cleaner mounted on top of the rocker cover added to its overall height, accounting, incidentally, for the noticeable slope of the bonnet top which was a characteristic of the type.

Continuing demand for the A173 7.7-litre unit led to the introduction of a variant of the Regal Mark III in which this engine and the equally familiar crash gearbox were mounted in a Mark III chassis, thus combining the main characteristics of the O662/20 with the appearance of the later model, and allowing standardisation of components. Also, a flexible engine mounting, as shown here, gave passengers a similar degree of quietness and reduced vibration with the 7.7-litre engine as was experienced with the 9.6, though the familiar gearbox whine was still clearly heard.

bodies in 1948), followed by Sheffield United (sixteen vehicles) and Maidstone & District (55 vehicles) though these two batches both included some not built until after the type prefix had become 6821A.

SMT, which had officially become Scottish Omnibuses Ltd from the beginning of 1948 but continued to use the previous initials as a trading name, placed 35 vehicles with chassis numbers O682084-118 into service between March and July of that year, all with Alexander bodywork but including some with more spacious seating for 30 passengers for use on long-distance services rather than the hitherto standard 35.

A second batch totalling 59 was split between Burlingham and Alexander bodywork, the former building nineteen buses, 20 coaches and one special 8ft.-wide coach with fully-fronted cab and concealed radiator exhibited at the 1948 Commercial Motor Show, while the latter supplied nineteen of its standard coach bodies which could perhaps be described as dual-purpose. This brought SMT's B series of fleet numbers up to B404, still the largest fleet of Regals outside London. Somewhat surprisingly the B-series carried on, being used for underfloor-engined Regal Mark IV and Reliance vehicles, as well as becoming more complex by the reissue of blank numbers for acquired vehicles, but up to B404, the fleet numbers issued could be taken as a reflection of SMT's purchases of

front-engined Regals, the only exceptions being two normal-control Rangers (mechanically similar to the Regal) and a 1929-type Reliance acquired with purchased businesses.

If at first the O682/6821A version of the Regal III was often the choice of the big company fleets, it did also have a following among independent operators who considered that they did not need the extra performance offered by the 9.6-litre engine and, in effect, wanted a mildly updated Regal I. Other concerns who tended to take a similar view included the Red & White group, which had tended to favour the 7.7-litre Regal for many of its post-war purchases as an alternative to its traditional Albion preferences, and some Tilling companies which no doubt favoured the 7.7-litre-engined AEC as an option to the Bristol L6A which also used the AEC 7.7.

Bearing in mind the continuance of the 27ft. 6in. limit on overall length for two-axle single-deckers operating in Britain until 1950, and the overall 30 mph speed limit for public service vehicles that was to persist for another decade, this preference for the smaller engine is understandable. However, the 9.6-litre engine was proving to be an even more durable engine than the widely respected '7.7', and there were applications where the preselective gearbox offered considerable advantages.

Thus, although BET had been unenthusiastic about the 9.6-plus-

preselective combination and, as a group, was generally turning away from it after 1948 deliveries, even where examples had been delivered, there were exceptions. Thus South Wales Transport Co Ltd began its first post-1945 single-deck deliveries in 1949 with 30 of the 6821A and eighteen of the 9621E types, the former for general duties and the latter for the arduous Townhill route in Swansea, for which a succession of non-standard vehicle types had been used previously. There were also a further three 9621E chassis with Windover coach bodywork. The 1950 intake was entirely crash-gearbox fitted, however, with nine more 6821A buses and seventeen of the 9621A version as coaches, again with Windover bodywork. Sheffield United split its contracts for coaches in 1949 and 1950, on both occasions taking both 7.7-litre and 9.6-litre versions, though in the latter case staying with the epicyclic gearbox both years.

Overseas orders continued to take a major part in Regal III sales. Some indication of the relative progress of alternative versions was given by the chassis numbers of examples on display at the 1948 Earls Court Show. These included 9621E434 for Enterprise of Scunthorpe, 6821A316 for Scottish Omnibuses, 9631E548 for Lisbon and 9631E859, a Park Royal-bodied example intended as a demonstrator for the South American market. The left-hand 9631E model was thus well in front, even if the demonstrator may have been completed more quickly than examples ordered by operators, which frequently had to take their time in lengthy waiting lists in those days of immense worldwide demand.

Many of the right-hand 962-series chassis built were also for export and even the 6821A model, not primarily intended for overseas sales, had some foreign buyers — among the last built being 6821A570-585 for Nordisk Dieselunto, the AEC agents in Copenhagen.

The home market was in fact about to virtually collapse with the advent of underfloor-engined models. It had been an open secret that AEC was developing such a vehicle and some operators, and in particular London Transport, delayed placing bulk orders for single-deckers in the knowledge that a new model was in the offing. It was announced as the Regal Mark IV at the end of 1949 and from then on the writing seemed to be on the wall for the Regal III, at any rate as a home-market chassis.

However, there were to be further versions of the Regal III even for use in the UK, and as an export model the type was to remain in production for about eight more years. The rigid standardisation of the 1946-47 period had long gone, and if a major operator wanted something out of the ordinary that did not disrupt production unduly, it was sometimes agreed. Thus Trent Motor Traction decided that a synchromesh gearbox would be desirable and hence 20 of the 7.7-litre-engined model were built with Crossley four-speed synchromesh units, the chassis numbers being 6821X428-447 and the vehicles entering service in 1950. Crossley Motors Ltd had been purchased by AEC in 1948 and although manufacture of complete Crossley vehicles was winding down by that date, Crossley units on sub-assemblies were being used on some AEC chassis until well into the 'fifties.

Another instance of this was on Regal III models which formed part of an order from Linjebuss, the Swedish operator involved in the Europabus international services, fulfilled in 1951. These included both left and right-hand drive models and an overdrive five-speed gearbox was required, so a Crossley-built unit was incorporated, the models in question being designated 9621R and 9631R.

The limitations on dimensions on vehicles for operation in Britain were relaxed in 1950, when the maximum length went up to 30ft. Although this was the intended overall length of the 20ft. wheelbase overseas chassis as built from 1946, it was unsuitable for this new home-market application because it could not meet UK turning circle requirements. So a new set of 19ft. 3in. wheelbase models was introduced, available in 9621E, 9621A and 6821A versions. As it turned out, sales of these were relatively limited as the majority of potential operators turned to the new Regal Mark IV underfloor-engined chassis. The 17ft. 6in. wheelbase models were still available, but sales of these, too, were limited.

Home-market sales after mid-1950 tended to be confined to the more conservatively-minded independent and municipal operators, the latter generally being among the smaller undertakings. The proportion of home-market sales of 962-series chassis became markedly less after about 1000 serial numbers had been issued. An analysis of sales up to March 1953, which was just about the date by which home-market sales had ceased, showed that 1,517 of the 962-model chassis had been produced for all markets, while the figure for the 963 left-hand version was 1,663 and exactly 600 of the 682 type with 7.7-litre engine.

Export emphasis

Export sales continued and began to take on a new character, with emphasis on the Regal III's suitability for operation where poor road surfaces or other factors made an amidships underfloor engine unsuitable. London Transport engineers were asked to advise a number of operators in the Middle East on the setting up of urban transport systems. AEC Mark III models were an understandable choice and Baghdad placed a succession of orders for left-hand Regal chassis with crash gearboxes, a combination not hitherto offered officially, and thus creating a model 9631A. The first 100 were built in 1951-52, another 100 in 1953 and the third and final batch again of 100 in 1955-56. All had Park Royal bodywork and they also bodied 20 double-deckers of similar specification in 1953 — although officially these were Regents, the lack of a model number for a left-hand Regent caused these also to be designated 9631A. Similar remarks applied to preselective gearbox double-decker chassis, though some were 9661E.

However, Africa also proved to be a sizeable market for Regal chassis in the mid-'fifties. In 1955, the Uganda Transport Co Ltd received 24 of the 9621E type, half of them 21ft. 6in. wheelbase and half 17ft. 6in. and a further 24, all of the long-wheelbase type, followed in 1956. Uganda Eastern Provinces Bus Co also took 40 examples in 1956.

Production of Regal Mark III chassis ended in December 1957, the final production figure for the O962 and 9621 series being 1,595, that for the O963 and 9631 (including limited numbers of Regent 9661) being 1,765, and for the O682 and 6821 being 734.

The Regal Mark V

The ending of Regal III production was not quite the end of vertical-engined Regals, as a Mark V version was announced in 1955. (The Mark IV had of course been the underfloor-engined version introduced in 1949-50, by then superseded as a home-market model though still current — and being built in quantity — for overseas.) The Regal Mark V was intended to bring the front-engined Regal into line with the contemporary Regent Mark V. Although derived from the Mark III and offered in left and right-hand versions with the same alternative wheelbase lengths, it brought in the so-called 'semi-automatic' form of epicyclic gearbox, with gear changes responding to movements of a control switch mounted on the steering column, in place of the previous preselective system.

The 11.3-litre engine derived from the 9.6-litre unit by increasing the cylinder bore by 10 mm, had become a popular choice in export markets and so the Regal Mark V incorporated it as standard. Designations were thus S2RA or S2LA, according to whether right or left-hand. A lighter version with the AV470 7.75-litre engine and a synchromesh gearbox — equivalent to the home-market medium-weight version of the Regent V — was also offered and designated MS3RV, although this only appeared in specification sheets briefly.

As it turned out, the continuation of the Regal III for a couple of years after it was officially obsolete delayed manufacture of the few Regal V models built. The first left-hand chassis, S2LA001, one of five for Luanda Municipality in Angola, was not bodied until May 1959. The type of customer for such vehicles often tended to favour a higher-framed chassis and AEC's sales swung over to the Ranger of this period, which was in effect a passenger version of the contemporary Mercury goods model or, in South Africa, the Kudu, with straight frame similar to that of the underfloor-engined Regal but with vertical engine at the front. So the front-engine Regal faded from the scene.

Not all countries where traffic keeps to the right wanted left-hand steering. AEC's first post-war passenger chassis exports to Norway were two O962-type Regal III models for Vagsbygd Ruta of Kristiansand placed in service in 1947. The locally-built bodywork incorporated passenger doors amidships and at the rear. Note the curved-glass corner window in the cab.

London Transport's final addition to its T class consisted of 30 Regal III models with Mann Egerton 31-seat bodywork for country bus duties, entering service between March and September 1948. The chassis were to standard 'Provincial' specification apart from a few minor London-style items and the bodywork was also of a curiously 'un-Chiswick-like' style. The later chassis were built after the changeover to the four-figure chassis prefix and so T797, the penultimate T-type, seen above in original green and white livery at Rickmansworth, and T791, seen right on Green Line relief duty at Amersham in 1956, were respectively 9621E182 and 177. At about the same date the front hub cap changed to a new flat-faced type with coloured AEC badge. These vehicles were classified 15T13.

In January 1948, the first of 50 Regal Mark III O963-type buses for the Buenos Aires Transport Board was inspected by the Argentine Ambassador in London before being shipped. The 35-seat bodywork was by Saunders Engineering Shipyard, a concern set up in Beaumaris, Anglesey, as an off-shoot of Saunders-Roe Ltd, the flying boat manufacturers and quite prominent as a bus bodybuilder in the early post-war period. Some 35 of their vehicles were diverted after arrival to a State-owned concern, Empresa Nacional 17 Octobre, operating on an inter-urban route from Buenos Aires.

The 7.7-litre version of the Regal Mark III was given little emphasis in AEC publicity but was popular with many company operators. This example was one of twelve supplied to Crosville Motor Services Ltd in 1948-49 at a period when the Tilling group, to which Crosville by then belonged, had relaxed its otherwise rigid standardisation policy based on the use of Bristol chassis and Eastern Coachworks bodies, both produced within the group, because of the availability of limited numbers of vehicles from other sources to help overcome the shortage of new rolling stock. One senses the relish with which Mr W. J. Crosland Taylor, of the family which had founded Crosville, took the opportunity as General Manager to depart from what he felt was a limitation on his freedom of action. He had always been primarily a Leyland devotee, but AEC vehicles were also respected. However, the Southern and Western National companies also took six similar Regals apiece and the entire batch received 35-seat bodywork built by Strachans to a style intended to resemble the contemporary ECW design. TA 9, on chassis number 6821A205, is seen leaving Llandudno Town depot in October 1949. The batch remained in service until 1961. The depot architecture is noteworthy.

The Great Northern Railway of Ireland placed 30 Regal III 9.6-litre fluid transmission models in service in 1948, its first Regals apart from a Mark II purchased in 1936, though there had been a sizeable fleet of Reliance buses dating from 1929 and several batches of Regents from 1937 onwards. The Regals were on 20ft.-wheelbase export chassis as Ireland permitted 30ft. overall length for two-axle vehicles, a dimension not permissible in the UK until 1950. Park Royal built the bodywork, one of the 24 which had 39-seat bus bodies on framing supplied by Metal Sections being seen nearing completion [right]. This picture clearly shows the bonnet design of the Mark III chassis, the top being hinged up by simply pushing against an over-centre spring system. The radiator was covered in adhesive tape to protect the chromium plating. The more sharply downward-turned Mark III type of dumb iron, normally hidden by the mudguard, is also visible. Below is shown No. 427, the first of the six 35-seat coaches of timber-framed construction. Unusually these had full-width canopies and the buses half-canopies rather than vice versa as was more normal at the time.

The GNR livery was an attractive combination of Oxford blue and cream but in 1959 the fleet was taken over by Coras Iompair Eireann. Withdrawal began in 1965.

Another European country to favour right-hand Regals was Denmark, where quite sizeable numbers of both the O662/20 and Mark III models [largely O682 and 6821A] were imported from 1946 until the early 'fifties. Many went to the Danish State Railway fleet but in February 1949, eight Regal III entered service with Nordsjael-lands Elektricitets og Sporvejs Aktieselskab of Hellerup near Copenhagen on a suburban service into that city. This concern also operated 20 B.U.T. trolleybuses.

In typical AEC fashion during the Rackham era, bodybuilders were persuaded to produce 'something special' for the Mark III passenger range. Most of this effort was concentrated on double-deckers with four-bay rather than the usual five-bay layout of the period but Duple did produce a corresponding version of its A-series body, code FS14, which also had wider than standard window bays as compared to the FS1, and was offered only on the Regal III. Here the direct comparison can be made in a view of vehicles owned by G. J. Miller & Sons of Cirencester. Nearest the camera is HAD 362, on chassis O962279 with fluid transmission and 35-seat FS14 body placed in service in May 1948. Behind is visible a Dennis Lancet III with FS1 body.

Some 28 AEC Regal III models, all with 9.6-litre engines and fluid transmission, were placed in service between 1947 and 1949 by Enterprise of Scunthorpe, mainly with Willowbrook 35-seat dual-purpose bodywork, as shown here on EFW 387 [O962414] seen when quite new, parked alongside the former Kings Cross coach station which was, regrettably, to remain fenced-off and never restored to its original use. When the Enterprise fleet was taken over by Lincolnshire Road Car Co Ltd in 1950, the management of the latter were reputed to be most impressed by the Regal III vehicles and it is said that a further order would have been placed had it not conflicted with Tilling group policy, once again wedded to standardisation on Bristol chassis.

[Below] 'Something special' was again no doubt the intention when the main Burlingham exhibit for the 1948 Commercial Motor Show was being devised. The Scottish Motor Traction Co Ltd was taking delivery of a batch of 59 7.7-litre-engined Regal III [6821A305-344, O682345-356 and 6821A357-363]. All but one of these were fitted with Alexander or Burlingham bodywork of conventional bus or coach styles [the latter could perhaps be classed as dual-purpose]. However, for the October 1948 Commercial Motor Show in London, chassis 6821A316 was built to 8ft. width [the remainder of SMT's fleet then being 7ft. 6in.] and fitted with a fully-fronted 33-seat coach body to this design, which was to remain unique, though some elements of later more familiar styles can, with hindsight, be recognised. It was beginning to be fashionable to

depart from recognisable radiator grilles in such designs, but perhaps the most curious feature was the narrowing of the body towards the front to accept what was not a particularly wide windscreen having no central division. B364 [GSC 457] is seen leaving St. Andrews Square, Edinburgh on the London route soon after entering service [which did not occur until June 1949, though the author can remember seeing it drive out of Earls Court immediately the Show closed]. It is leading B157, a 1935 Regal [O6621650] which had been newly rebodied by Alexander to the style also being used for new Regal chassis. B364 was withdrawn in 1962, although it spent a further year with the associated Highland fleet. Its seating capacity was reduced to 31 before entering service but increased to 35 in 1958/9.

[Above] The Regal III could, however, be a basis for exceptionally good-looking vehicles in a more 'classic' mould. Mansfield District was still maintaining its traditional allegiance to the Regal-Weymann combination and took delivery of some 24 vehicles of the 9621E type in 1949, the first single-deckers for this fleet [apart from a couple of wartime experimental articulated vehicles with Commer tractive units] since 1940. No. 25 on chassis 9621E497 is seen posed just outside the gates to AEC's Southall factory before delivery. The seating capacity was 35. This was almost the end of the road for such additions to the fleet, for both Midland General and Mansfield District were soon to adopt Tilling-group vehicle policies after being taken over by the then British Transport Commission.

[Below] The Duple D-series bus body looked if anything even better on the Regal III chassis than it had on the Regal I. This example for Gelly-gaer Urban District Council was posed at almost the same spot, but viewed in the opposite direction, in June 1950. No. 11 was one of four 35-seat buses of this type on the crash-gearbox 9621A version of the chassis with its somewhat incongruous 'vintage vehicle' sound effects, this being 9621A958. The economics of a bus requiring a crew of two with so small a capacity would seem impossible in these days when one-man double-deckers often fail to pay their way but bus travel was nearing an all-time peak and good loadings could virtually be guaranteed at most times of day.

In 1950, a length of 30ft. became permissible for two-axle single-deckers in Britain and the 8ft. width previously confined to specific individually approved routes, became generally allowable; accordingly the Regal III was made available in 19ft. 3in. wheelbase form. This example for Surrey Motors Ltd was photographed before delivery in March 1951. As usual for this operator, Harrington built the bodywork which gave quite spacious seating for 35 passengers. Despite the increased dimensions, this operator favoured the 7.7-litre engine and this model was still designated 6821A. However, demand for home-market Regal III coaches dropped sharply on the arrival of the Regent IV and such vehicles were comparatively rare.

A major boost to overall sales of the Regal III, arriving just as home-market demand was dropping, was a contract from Baghdad Passenger Transport Service in Iraq for 100 vehicles. They were outwardly almost a mirror image of a home-market bus, being on 17ft. 6in. wheelbase chassis. London Transport officials had advised on the city's transport needs and the choice of AEC chassis and Park Royal bodywork, as well as some minor details of the body design, such as the horizontal division of the side panels for ease of repair, reflected LT influence. However, the chassis had crash gearboxes, and in the photograph on the left, taken in October 1951, the rather complex mechanism to combine this with left-hand drive is just visible on chassis awaiting bodying. The type 9631A chassis was a new variant not previously available. Two repeat orders, for a further 100 vehicles on each occasion, were fulfilled in 1953 [of which an example is shown below] and 1956-57.

Virtually the end of the line for home-market Regal III models came in the spring of 1953, when Doncaster Corporation took delivery of three 9621A 19ft. 3in. wheelbase chassis with appropriately traditional-looking 39-seat Roe bodywork. Sales had already dwindled to a trickle and 9621A1590 is sometimes claimed as the last home Regal III, but Gellygaer UDC did not take delivery of 9621A1583 and 4 until 1954.

Export sales, notably to Africa, continued however, and this delightful photograph shows one of twelve Park Royal-bodied 21ft. 6in. wheelbase 9621E models built for the Uganda Transport Co Ltd towards the end of 1955 well and truly laden not long after entering service. This was built as a 70-seat bus, but there were probably 100 passengers aboard and the total gross weight seems bound to have been well above the 14½ tons gross maximum for which this version of the model was designed. Understandably, another photograph taken on the same occasion was used on the front cover on a leaflet for the recently-introduced Regal V published in August 1956.

This chassis drawing shows the 21ft. 6in. wheelbase version of the Regal V model S2RA, which differed from the corresponding Regal III 9612E in little other than having Monocontrol semi-automatic gearbox. This version of the chassis retained the traditional exposed radiator and bonnet layout designed for half-cab bodywork, though the lighter MS3RV version had the so-called semi-full-front as used on most Regent V double-deckers and, in practice, a version of the S2 chassis to suit fully-fronted bodywork was produced for Luanda Municipality [see 'Park Royal Coachworks Vol. 2', page 107]. The drawing is reproduced to a scale of 4mm to 1ft.

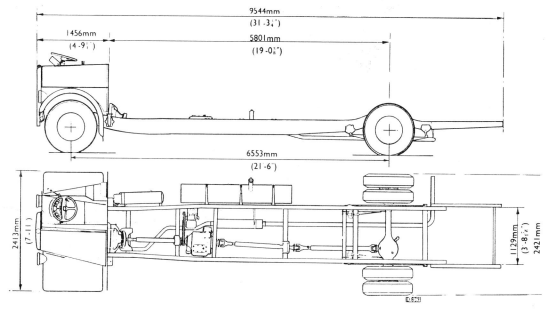

An indication of the step forward in design represented by the Regal is conveyed by this view taken in the works in the 1929-30 period. An early production Regal, ready for delivery to the bodybuilders, looks graceful and modern when seen against a background of chassis, also new but belonging to the previous design generation. Admittedly they mostly appear to be 418 goods models but they convey the general appearance of a typical AEC of the 'twenties, which did not differ greatly from the concepts of the pre-1914 era.

Chapter Eight : Front-engined Regals in retrospect

The market position of the original Regal as introduced in 1929 was much the same as that of the Leyland Tiger first seen a couple of years earlier. On the one hand, it was two years behind in establishing its position, and its penetration of many major company fleets was limited simply because the Tiger was already there and already establishing a good reputation. On the other hand, Rackham had been able to make a significant step forward in front-end layout and appearance and the Regal made almost everything else on the market at the beginning of the 1930 season look dated.

Independent operators, always conscious of the need to be up-to-date reacted to this and the Regal soon became established as an attractive chassis on which to base stylish coach work, while yet retaining the combination of performance, refinement and reliability of the Tiger. By the mid-'thirties, the Tiger and other competitors had caught up in this respect. Regal sales, though never stationary, were for a time not so buoyant and the ventures into the Regal 4 four-cylinder model and later the Regal Mark II lightweight version were not particularly successful.

However, the idea of rebodying early chassis, which began to get under way with the Tiger from about 1935, as indicated in 'Best of British Buses No.3', was applied with, if anything, even more enthusiasm to the Regal. Up to 1937, a 1930 Regal chassis looked almost indistinguishable from the current product and as this was still among the better-looking models of the period, a rebodied early Regal looked almost exactly like a new coach. The cynic might even suggest that the face-lift applied in mid-1937, with lengthened radiator, modified mudguards, etc was intended partly to encourage the coach operator to buy new rather than rebodying an existing Regal. This would be an exaggeration, of course, but rebodying early Regals was carried out on quite a big scale. When London Transport began to sell off much of its original Green Line fleet, plus other Regals acquired from independents, many started a second lease of life with smart new bodywork.

Meanwhile, new production had perked up with the advent of more suitable and efficient oil engines. The 1938 Green Line fleet had nicely settled down, building a reputation

as impressive in that period as had the previous 1930-31 vehicles, but the war brought Green Line services to an abrupt and, in retrospect, somewhat unreasonable halt.

The 10T10 vehicles spent the war period on non-passenger duties, notably as 'Clubmobiles' dispensing refreshmeent to the US Army stationed in Britain and required extensive renovation before they were fit for Green Line use again.

Elsewhere, some Regals were rebuilt during wartime, the SMT coach fleet of 1933-34 being rebuilt on Regent frames as double-deckers. As the war ended, rebodying and rebuilding activities intensified as a means of overcoming the shortage of new vehicles caused by the war despite massive production of new chassis. The interchangeablility of components within the 662 series of Regal models made it possible to fit even the earliest chassis not only with a current A173 7.7-litre engine but, if desired, the latest style of radiator and mudguards. Some of these rebuilds were so extensive and made up of units from a variety of sources that the original identity was lost. The Don Everall concern produced quite sizeable numbers of such rebuilds for its own fleet and others, for example and Morley's Grey Coaches of Mildenhall, Suffolk was another prolific producer of Regal rebuilds.

Meanwhile, the standard post-war Regal I was to be seen in fleets all over the country. It was no longer the last word in modern design (though it still looked well among another generation of contemporaries), but was regarded more as a work-horse. The Regal Mark III, especially in the original standard form with 9.6-litre engine and preselective gearbox, was a different story. The author recalls a journey across the south of County Durham around 1947-48 when the bus in which he was travelling, a 1946 Regal I of one of the independent operators, broke down with a fuel pump defect and a brand new Regal III coach was brought out as the changeover vehicle. The contrast in smoothness and, to catch up with the timetable, performance was immense.

The preselective Regal III made an impressive coach, far more refined than a Leyland PS1 for instance, and many examples went on being treated as the pride of independent operators' fleets until the change-over to underfloor engines made them too dated to keep in top-flight service. Many operators fought shy of fluid flywheels and epicyclic gearboxes in those days — notably the BET group — and the crash gear-box version was produced to meet this attitude. Unfortunately the marriage of the 9.6-litre engine and this 1931-design gearbox was not particularly happy. Some gearbox failures occurred but even when no specific trouble was experienced, the overall effect was rather dated, particularly in sound effects, attractive though they may now appear to old-vehicle enthusiasts. The 7.7-litre Regal III was perhaps a more consistent specification and could be considered as a mildly updated Regal I, gaining in quietness from the flexible engine mounting, even if

Sidney Camm's famous comment about aeroplane design — ''if it looks right, it probably is right'' — certainly applied to the Regal, of which the frontal appearance set a standard for others to copy. This 1931 example, 662979, was one of a batch of 20 supplied to East Midland Motor Services Ltd, one of the first major company users of the model. Brush built the bodywork which was to BET Federation design, this vehicle LC20 [registered VO 5620] being one of three with 30-seat coach interiors. The taller than usual radiator filler was briefly favoured by some companies, including the London General Omnibus Co, around that time.

still plagued by an irritating transmission-line 'grumble' when cruising at say 30 mph.

However, the days of the front-engined single-decker were numbered and between 1950 and 1953 the Regal III slipped from being one of the leading models of its day into

a rarity and virtual extinction. It lived on for several more years abroad latterly in Mark V form, but by 1959 this era of the Regal was over. Thirty years had passed since it was introduced during which the name was one of the most respected in the industry.

Numerous Regal chassis were rebodied over the years. One of the first was one of the Green Line coaches of the 1931 batch, T232. This had been damaged in an accident. The opportunity was taken to fit a Weymann metal-framed body — actually the second to be built under the newly-formed arrangement which enabled Weymann to use Metropolitan-Cammell's constructional methods as part of the deal which set up Metropolitan-Cammell Weymann [better known as MCW]. The vehicle thus rebodied re-entered service in April 1933, considerably modernised in appearance, although the windowless cab door reflected continued conservatism on such matters. No further bodywork of this style was produced, but Weymann metal-framed designs were to be a frequent choice for the 'green' London Transport country fleet set up later that year. As it happened, T232 was rebodied again in June 1938, with a 1935 body, again by Weymann, similar to that shown overleaf.

Regals taken over with acquired businesses added substantially to the ex-LGOC and Green Line fleet which London Transport more directly 'inherited' on its formation in 1933. Representative was T366 [KX 8644], which was among the newest vehicles in the combined fleet, having entered service in May 1932 — its chassis number was 6621351. It was taken over from Amersham & District in November 1933 and had thus somewhat resembled KX 6785, as shown on page 21, until repainted in Green Line livery — the 32-seat body was by Strachans. It is seen here still 'at home' outside Amersham garage from which it continued to operate on the service into London.

London Transport was an early protagonist of the philosophy of fitting up-to-date bodywork to Regal chassis. Twelve of the ex-independent chassis dating from 1930-31, T346-357, were sent to Weymann in 1935 for new metal-framed bodywork to London Transport's design and bearing an obvious relationship to contemporary STL-type double-deck practice in such details as the cab [with windscreen pillars suitably curved to suit the single-deck profile, then a novel idea]. Seating capacity was originally only 26 and this photograph of T355, a former Queen Line vehicle, reveals that some, at least, were originally lettered for operation on Green Line service although generally considered as country buses — the seating capacity was later increased to 30. There seems little doubt that had London Transport placed any new single-deck buses on Regal chassis in the mid to late 'thirties, they would have looked very much like this, save perhaps that the 'tight-fitting' nearside front mudguard would have given way to a standard STL-type [in fact the type shown seems to have been replaced soon after delivery]. Surprisingly, these vehicles were not converted to oil engines, though subsequent conversions, using similar bodies that had also been built in 1935 on Reliance chassis but were transferred mainly to 1931 ex-Green Line chassis in 1938, received 7.7-litre engines. All twelve went to the War Department for service in Germany in 1945 and did not return.

Many of London Transport's T-class coaches from the 1930-32 period were sold in 1938-39 and the ex-Amersham vehicle shown at the top of the page, KX 8644, was among many that went to Arlington Motor Co, the north London dealers, in this case in February 1939. New Duple coach bodywork was fitted and it was sold to Clarke of Canning Town, E16, remaining with that concern for nearly a decade apart from some years in wartime with the Royal Navy. By the time this photograph was taken at Epsom in 1950, it had been operated for a year by Overland Coaches of Kentish Town, NW5, and had acquired post-war style front wings and radiator.

[Above] Many of the companies under Tilling management adopted a policy of fitting new bodywork on old chassis in the 'thirties. This had been done before, but the idea of updating the vehicles to make them almost indistinguishable from new had not previously been carried through to its logical conclusion. In 1937, United Automobile Services Ltd gave the full treatment to seven Regals dating from 1930-31 and acquired from independent coach operators; they received new bodywork by Eastern Coach Works to the same 35-seat style as was being fitted to new Bristol JO5G chassis, and also new AEC 7.7-litre engines. These three had all been placed in service in May 1931 by Phillipsons Motor Coaches Ltd, which concern, though having a London address, registered most of its vehicles in York. Newly renumbered ARO 6, 4 and 3, VY 2552, 2551 and 2784 were respectively on chassis 662828, 662643 and 662958. They were photographed at AEC's Southall works, probably having gone to the service department there after rebodying to receive the new engines. Naughtily, 'AEC Gazette' reproduced the picture in its regular 'new deliveries' feature, no doubt seeking to give the impression that United was still buying new AEC buses, though in fairness five new coaches were delivered that year [see page 57]. The rebodied vehicles remained in service, generally on routes in the Northumberland area, until 1950-53, having gone through a complex series of renumberings.

[Below] This picture, widely used for many years in publicity for Royal Blue coach services, was taken shortly after LJ 1519, one of the batch originally delivered to Elliott Bros Ltd in 1930, had been fitted with a new 32-seat body by Beadle in 1939. The vehicle had passed to Western National ownership in 1935 after the takeover of the Elliott business, becoming WNOC No. 3631, but continued as a Royal Blue vehicle, like all those transferred to Western or Southern National. All were rebodied in the 1936-39 period, although two then ceased to be Royal Blue coaches, passing to the companies' 'own' coach fleets in cream and green livery. The body style was very like that used for new Royal Blue coaches from the beginning of the Western and Southern National period of which the first examples had been built on Bristol J chassis by Eastern Counties, though there were sixteen new Regals with Mumford or Duple bodies in 1937. This particular vehicle was severely damaged in an air raid in August 1943 and was subsequently scrapped, but others were still regularly to be seen on Royal Blue services between London and the South West until the early 1950's.

By the mid-'thirties Regals were to be found in most continents. This photograph, taken in Johannesburg in August 1938 shows a 19ft. wheelbase petrol-engined example operated by Johnston Bus Service of Germiston, an operator which had adopted the AEC Q for more recent orders at that date [see 'Best of British Buses' No. 2, page 72]. Note the short rear overhang and the high-mounted semaphore-type direction indicator.

[Below] Although Crosville standardised on Leylands in the 'thirties, AEC Regals which came into the fleet were sufficiently highly regarded for all the fifteen examples [all petrol-engined] which were in the fleet in 1939 to be sent to Eastern Coach Works for new 32-seat bodies of a style officially described as 'semi-coach'. The example shown was the oldest, being on chassis number 662015 and having been exhibited at the 1929 Commercial Motor Show with its original Harrington 21-seat coach body. It was supplied to the LMS Railway, being registered in Watford [as usual for LMS road vehicles] as UR 6300, but almost immediately transferred to Crosville. It remained in service until 1951. The comparison with a similarly rebodied Leyland Tiger shown on page 75 of 'Best of British' No. 5 ['75 years of Crosville'] reveals the more modern appearance of the Regal chassis though this body suited both designs particularly well.

Maidstone & District Motor Services Ltd was another operator to standardise on the Leyland Tiger as a basis for its coach fleet throughout the 'thirties. However, a number of Regals were acquired, most notably as a result of the takeover of Autocar Services Ltd in 1933, following the reorganisation of services along the fringes of the M & D area as a result of the formation of London Transport. Autocar had been part of the LGOC empire and thus its 21 Regals had been allocated the fleet numbers T325-345, but the transfer to M & D meant that they did not come into the London Transport fleet. Thus KR 9916, new in May 1931, had been T342 but from 1933 became M & D's No. 49. The original LGOC-style Park Royal body was replaced in 1946 by the Harrington 32-seat front-entrance coach body shown, of the characteristic style built specifically for this operator between 1935 and 1949. Some 116 new Regal I [O662/20] and III [O682 or 6821A], mostly with the same type of body, entered service in 1947-49.

[Above] Most of the pictures in this book show Regals either sparkling new or well-cared-for, but in the war years few operators were able to maintain normal standards. This picture, taken in September 1941, shows how battered some vehicles became as a result of minor scrapes, often occurring during the blackout when the masked headlamps gave only the merest glimmer of light, lack of staff to carry out repairs and, in this case, intensive use serving construction and operation of RAF airfields. Yeomans Motors, of Canon Pyon, Hereford, had placed VJ 7405, on chassis 6621727 with Duple 32-seat body, in service new in 1935.

The Devon General Omnibus & Touring Co Ltd's 1938, 1939 and 1940 batches of Regals had been among the most elegant of all examples of the model with bus bodywork when delivered new [see 'Blue Triangle', page 126]. Inevitably, wartime grey paint — in this case quite a dark shade, relieved only by the patch of normal crimson bearing the fleetname — dims the effect, though SR 439 on chassis O6623319, new in 1939, was still an attractive vehicle when photographed in 1943. Harrington built the 35-seat bodywork. The vehicle remained in service until 1952.

London Transport's 10T10 series of Green Line coaches of 1938-39 spent the war period 'on active service' of one type or another. Some 55 were placed at the disposal of the American Red Cross for conversion to 'Clubmobiles', which was a typically enterprising name given to the American equivalent of the more mundane-sounding mobile canteen, although rather more comprehensively equipped than most, with sleeping accommodation for the staff. They were all named after states or cities, 'Arkansas' being in reality T632 which like many others of the type had spent the early part of the war equipped, but little used, as an ambulance until handed to the ARC in February 1943. It was returned to LT in November 1945 re-entering service some months later.

In wartime, AEC's works transport fleet included this Regal Mark II with goods bodywork which took advantage of the low-loading possibilities of the chassis. The identity of the chassis is not certain but it is believed to have been 862070, originally supplied to F. C. Cotton, who revived the common practice in the early days of coach operation of fitting a coach body in summer and a lorry body in winter. In the 'thirties this was most unusual, and by the war period the vehicle had found its way back to AEC, by then permanently a lorry, where it remained into the post-war period.

[Above] Nominally, this SMT double-decker was a Regal, since it retained the registration number FS 8543 and chassis number O6621596 of the 1934 vehicle, fleet number B83, from which its main mechanical units were transferred. It was, in fact, a wartime rebuild, directly comparable to those of Leyland Tiger TS7 to Titan TD4 specification carried out on a much larger scale by the then SMT group. The parent company converted eighteen Regal coaches dating from 1933-34 which had operated on the London service and were out of service due to war-time cessation of long-distance operation, using new Regent frames but retaining their 8.8-litre engines and preselective gearboxes. SMT had no Regents until two of the so-called 'unfrozen' batch were allocated in 1942 and numbered BB1 and 2, so the rebuilds took the succeeding numbers BB3 to 20, BB11 being seen here. They had Alexander 53-seat bodies to wartime utility specification like those on the TS7 rebuilds and having a distinct touch of Leyland practice in their styling. BB11 remained in service until 1957. A 1948 Regent III with similar body is overtaking in this post-war picture — on the right is H250, one of the 1940 batch of 39-seat Tiger TS8 Specials.

Vehicles often tended to lose their original registration numbers if commandered for military service during the war and not returned to their original owners [who often declined them when in poor condition]. With no record of their original log book, subsequent owners tended to re-register as the simplest solution. Hence this Duple-bodied Regal, chassis number 6621520, dating from about 1933, received the registration FPT 356 when placed in service by Cosy Coaches of Meadowfield, County Durham in the latter part of the war period. It had been sold to a West Hartlepool operator, L & P, when photographed in 1947.

Wartime or early post-war rehabilitation was often a matter of drastic action to get vehicles back on the road rather than anything approaching either restoration to original condition or an attempt at modernisation. Thus Bath Tramways 2235 [GL 1510], on chassis 6621627, looked as if it dated from considerably earlier than 1934, which was when its chassis had been built, in this photograph taken in the late 'forties. Its original Park Royal body had been replaced in 1944 by one built by Eastern Counties from a 1932 Tilling-Stevens, one of a number acquired by Bath's parent Bristol Tramways & Carriage Co Ltd from the West Yorkshire Road Car Co Ltd in 1942. The cab had been modified to fit the AEC chassis and the destination display altered and in the process its appearance considerably altered. However, the mudguards, though quite possibly original, had been trimmed back perhaps to eliminate dents or rusted edges, giving them a look of the 'twenties. On the other hand, a 7.7-litre oil engine had been fitted and a touch characteristic of Tilling group fleets was the quick-acting inclined radiator filler cap of the type standard on new Bristol vehicles. The vehicle was withdrawn in 1950.

Conversely, this vehicle, though outwardly appearing to be a standard early post-1945 Regal I, was in reality 6621357, originally registered JH 1916 when first placed in service as a Harrington-bodied coach by the Lewis Omnibus Co Ltd of Watford in 1932. It was operated by London Transport as T368 from October 1933 until sold to Lancashire Motor Traders in May 1938. It then passed through two other operators' hands before being acquired in 1948 by Brunt's Coaches of Hatfield, Hertfordshire, rebuilt largely to O662/20 specification, fitted with new Duple body and re-registered KNK 510.

This line-up photographed in 1950, was even more remarkable, for all but the left-hand two of the vehicles were very different in origin to what they seemed. Morley's Grey Coaches Ltd of Mildenhall, Suffolk, was unable to obtain delivery of sufficient new Regals in the 1947-49 period and adopted a policy of purchasing AEC chassis and rebuilding. From left to right, the vehicles were CGV 218, a 1950 Regal III [9621E1232] with Gurney Nutting 37-seat body; BGV 754, also a 1949 Regal III [9621E760] with Plaxton 33-seat body; the remaining vehicles were all rebuilds to near O662/20 specification with new Duple bodies, as follows: BGV 3, based on a 1930 Regent originally WL 9069 ex-City of Oxford ['O661122']; BGV 648, originally a Regal demonstrator HX 1270 ['O662333']; BGV 1, another ex-Oxford Regent, originally WL 9077 ['O661110']; BGV 222 was originally an East Surrey vehicle PG 7840, later running as London T397 ['O662157'] and BCF 284 originally a Keith & Boyle coach of 1931 ['O662862']. The chassis numbers are as quoted after rebuild — originally they did not have the 'O' prefix.

More conventional rebodying was carried out on quite a large scale, however. The Trent Motor Traction Co Ltd had placed its first new Regals in service in 1937 and reverted to AEC for new vehicle requirements in 1946-50, after a period when Daimler [and for a time BMMO, built by Midland Red] had been in favour as chassis supplier. Having transferred some existing coach bodies [removed from Daimler chassis converted to double-deckers in wartime] to new Regal chassis in 1946, the opposite took place in 1950, when sixteen of the 1937 Regals received new Willowbrook bus bodies, including No. 714, on chassis O6622059, shown here. Like most of this batch, it had preselective transmission.

Perhaps the most remarkable instance of rebodying was the final stage of the programme covering most of its pre-war Regals carrried out by SMT [which had officially become Scottish Omnibuses Ltd in 1949, but still used the old initials until 1960]. The Burlingham Seagull body originally introduced for underfloor-engined chassis in 1950 had become available in front-engined form and was chosen in 1952 to rebody fifteen Regals dating from between 1935 and 1940. By that date it was possible to increase their original overall length and thus these vehicles seated 37 passengers. The oldest, B141 [WS 4489] on chassis O6621672 which dated from June 1935 is seen [left] — it remained in service until 1964, thus being 29 years old when withdrawn. Below are seen B230 [DSC 317] new in 1940, and B187 [BSC 524] of 1938 leading a convoy of similarly rebodied coaches in tour near Kinlochleven in the 'fifties.

Although always basically a single-decker chassis, the Regal was used as a basis for a few 1½-decker vehicles of one type or another, over the years. This example, photographed in December 1930, was publicised as being built by Oswald Tillotson Ltd but was in fact a Burlingham-bodied vehicle — the characteristic Blackpool Tower transfer is clearly visible just ahead of the rear mudguard. The front end of the body — described as was common at the time as an 'Observation coach' — was basically of standard Burlingham design.

Very few Regals of similar layout were produced in the intervening years before this example, different in styling but essentially the same in principle, was built on a Regal III 9621E chassis for Knight of Northampton in 1949. The fully-fronted cab had come into renewed favour, but this body, built by James Whitson of West Drayton, was relatively unusual at that date in retaining the traditional radiator. Whitson had built mainly on Maudslay chassis in the 1947-48 period.

Officially called a half-decker, the Crellin-Duplex body design with interlaced 'compartment' layout on two levels was an ingenious attempt to increase seating capacity in a vehicle of only slightly greater overall height than a single-decker. The same principle was used in a so-called double-deck electric suburban train operated by Southern Region of British Rail in the same period. This coach was for Granville Tours of Grimsby and was built on a 9621E chassis in 1950. Aside from its intriguing layout, its frontal appearance was hardly elegant.

The author prefers to close this volume with a more traditional Regal. Operated for its entire commercial life by Provincial of Leicester, JF 2378, dating from 1931 was acquired for preservation by the London Bus Preservation Group and is seen when taking part in the 1973 Historic Commercial Vehicle Club London-Brighton run. The bodywork is by Burlingham.

Acknowledgements

Once again, I can think of dozens, perhaps hundreds, of people who indirectly contributed to the pool of knowledge built up over about 40 years from which the information in this book is drawn; far too many to list even if I could remember all their names. Among them are some of my colleagues from AEC during my days there — some, sadly, no longer with us such as E. J. (John) Smith and my section leader in the drawing office when I joined the firm in 1951, Ray Martin. Happily, others have been able to tell me more in recent times, notably F. J. Sloan, who was able to provide such valuable background information on the late 'twenties and early 'thirties, while Bill Jardine produced a valuable collection of source material.

Among others, Mr Charles Hall was kind enough to recount the story of his family's Regal coach, shown on page 40, while Gavin Booth supplied a number of prints of Regals operating in Scotland. Jim Whiting, of Capital Transport, supplied most of the pictures of early Green Line coaches. Although much of the notes on individual vehicles come from the author's archives or memories, due credit must be given to the dedicated work of Omnibus Society and PSV Circle members. Last, but not least, the co-operation of Leyland Vehicles Ltd and its staff is much appreciated.

Photo Credits

Leyland Vehicles Ltd, except as follows:-

J. M. Aldridge	79(bottom)
Walter Alexander & Co (Coachbuilders) Ltd	58(top),71(top)
G. F. Ashwell	48(top)
Brush Coachworks Ltd	87(top)
C. R. L. Coles	52(top)
Crosville Motor Services Ltd	80(bottom)
Eastern Coachworks Ltd	90(centre)
R.N. Hannay	94(top)
D. W. K. Jones	18(all),19, 87(bottom),88(top)
London Transport Executive	59(both),70(top)
Metropolitan-Cammell Weymann Ltd	37(bottom), 65(bottom), 88(centre)
R. A. Mills	64(bottom)
D. Morris	92(centre)
S.A. Newman	93(centre)
J. Pettie	74(centre)
F. G. Reynolds	79(centre)
J. A. Senior	Front cover
Scottish Omnibuses Ltd	82(bottom),94(centre and bottom)
A. Townsin	74(bottom), 82(both top),92(bottom),95 (bottom)
A. Townsin collection	88(bottom),93(top)
J. E. Turley	90(bottom)